T0157233

Oracle
Recovery Appliance
Handbook

Oracle
Recovery Appliance
Handbook

An Insider's Insight

R A M E S H   R A G H A V

ORACLE RECOVERY APPLIANCE HANDBOOK
AN INSIDER'S INSIGHT

iUniverse books may be ordered through booksellers or by contacting:

iUniverse
1663 Liberty Drive
Bloomington, IN 47403
www.iuniverse.com
1-800-Authors (1-800-288-4677)

ISBN: 978-1-4917-9278-0 (sc)
ISBN: 978-1-4917-9277-3 (e)

Library of Congress Control Number: 2016905978

Print information available on the last page.

iUniverse rev. date: 4/28/2016

This book is dedicated to the unparalleled spiritual heritage of India.

PREFACE

I have always been amazed by the power of Oracle RMAN with all its rich functionality and deep database integration.

The Recovery Appliance, a new Engineered System from Oracle really fascinates me as it is the culmination of the best of Oracle's recovery technologies in a single rack.

I am truly indebted to Donna Cooksey, the Recovery Appliance Global Sales Enablement Lead at Oracle Corporation who helped me in numerous ways to get this book project going.

I am grateful to my wife Veena & son Yogindra for their support.

I extend my sincere thanks to the entire iUniverse team for getting this book published in accordance with my specifications.

Oracle Corporation's goal with the ZDLRA is to provide for simple and centralized backup and recovery of mission-critical databases. Designed to provide the highest protection for Oracle databases, this appliance delivers near-zero data loss data protection, minimal impact to end users, and a modern cloud-based architecture.

This book is for Oracle Database Administrators and Enterprise Architects responsible for data protection and business continuity. Readers should have a good understanding of Oracle database operation and architecture, especially with respect to backup and recovery.

References:

docs.oracle.com
IBM Tivoli Storage Manager for Databases, Data Protection for Oracle, Version 7.1
Symantec NetBackup for Oracle Administrator's Guide Release 7.6
RA product management site (Oracle internal)

CONTENTS

1

Introduction to RA

The *Zero Data Loss Recovery Appliance (ZDLRA)*, also called the *Recovery Appliance*, is a brand new Engineered System from Oracle Corporation. It has a fundamentally different approach to data protection. This enterprise level system can be used to backup and recover thousands of Oracle databases. The Recovery Appliance virtually eliminates data loss with its revolutionary design. It also offloads the overheads of backup and recovery from database servers. Tightly integrated with the intelligent Recovery Manager (RMAN), the Recovery Appliance is the heart of a centralized data protection strategy built around the paradigm of incremental-forever backup strategy. It is also ideally suited for the Cloud, with the extreme performant Exadata hardware under the covers.

In this chapter we will review the current unresolved issues in the backup and recovery space for Oracle databases. We will then learn how the brand new Recovery Appliance solution can address these various problems. We will then conclude with a brief overview of Exadata architecture.

So what are the pressing problems we have now for backing up and recovering Oracle databases?

Critical Data Protection Challenges:

- Exponential data growth with ever increasing backup windows exacerbating resource consumption issues on production servers

- Hundreds or Thousands of databases running on various platforms

- Continuous database availability to provide 24/7 access across multiple global time zones

- Absence of database backup validation for third-party backup snapshot and deduplication appliances

- Lack of end-to-end visibility in the database backup/recovery ecosystem with no clarity of status of backups, recoverability of databases etc.

So one may ask - what about the backup strategy using incrementally updated copies on disk? Here we are referring to the Recovery Manager (RMAN) technique of daily incremental backups, merging them into the full database copy. This this database copy is "rolled forward" continually. The RMAN code snippet below is an example of the above strategy:

RUN

{ RECOVER COPY OF DATABASE

WITH TAG 'merge_backup'

UNTIL TIME 'SYSDATE - 31';

BACKUP

INCREMENTAL LEVEL 1

FOR RECOVER OF COPY WITH TAG 'merge_backup' DATABASE; }

For large multi-terabyte databases the disk space needed for this method of backups would pose major challenges as full physical copies of database have to reside on disk and these would also expand in size due to incremental updates. Needless to say these database copies cannot be compressed as well.

In the current database backup scenarios the database host performs bulk of the backup/recovery processing. Agents for tape backup, deduplication etc. will be consuming resources on the host. Also backup compression, validation, deletion and other operations add to resource crunch on the database server.

We can conclude all the prevailing technologies fail to provide a performant, holistic and fool proof data protection solution for Oracle databases.

Enter the Zero Data Loss Recovery Appliance (ZDLRA) from Oracle Corporation!

This Recovery Appliance (RA) virtually eliminates data loss, offloads all chores associated with backup/restore from production database servers and also provides end-to-end visibility in the database backup ecosystem. And it can scale up & out on demand. So now we can effectively backup **AND** recover thousands of databases across the enterprise as well as in the Cloud.

What does RA offer in the backup/ recovery space?

- Dramatically reduced backup/recovery windows: The one and ONLY backup operation running on the database hosts is the one to send incremental backups to the Recovery Appliance. In an incremental-forever strategy, only one incremental level 0 backup is required in the lifetime of each data file to 'seed' the RA. After that the Recovery Appliance automatically validates, indexes, compresses and writes to disk, each (cumulative) incremental level 1 backup received from the database hosts. Below is an example of this strategy:

BACKUP CUMULATIVE INCREMENTAL LEVEL 1

DEVICE TYPE sbt FORMAT '%d_%U' TAG '%TAG' DATABASE;

The Recovery Appliance employs virtual full backups that are created on-demand for restore and recovery. A virtual full backup is a complete database image as of a certain point in time. This enables very fast restore and recovery operations. The incremental-forever strategy is a great mechanism to shorten the backup/recovery windows significantly.

- Elimination of data loss: The RA receives real-time redo transport from the databases like in a Data Guard configuration. The databases ship redo blocks from memory asynchronously to this appliance which are then written to the staging area. An added advantage that accrues here is further shortening of backup windows as we do not need to backup archived logs separately on the database hosts. The pre-installed Oracle Secure Backup software and the optional Fiber Channel cards can be used for performing tape archival. (read NO expensive third party media manager licences!) However you may still deploy tape backup agents from third-party vendors like Tivoli or NetBackup on the Recovery Appliance. The backups may also be replicated to a downstream RA for further protection.

- End-to-End Data Validation: How do we know our database backups are in good shape? We have to validate and perform restore/recovery successfully on a frequent basis. Corruptions will invalidate backups and render them useless. Obviously this will endanger data availability. The Recovery Appliance automatically validates the backups being ingested before writing to disk. Also, the integrity of the backups in the RA storage is periodically checked. Since Oracle ASM is used for RA storage, the mirrored copy can automatically be used to repair corrupted blocks on the primary if needed. The Exadata storage software automatically performs disk scrubbing periodically when the workload is very low. This is used to repair bad sectors on the disks. Recovery Appliance validates backup blocks on copy to tape and also when restoring them from tape. The downstream Recovery Appliance if configured, also validates blocks during the backup ingest and restore phases.

- Total control: Enterprise Manager 12c (Cloud Control) provides a "single pane of glass" view of the entire backup/recovery ecosystem. Metrics like backup performance, storage consumption etc. are easily captured. Also alerts are raised for any backup or Recovery Appliance issues. Recovery Appliance also can scale on demand to support thousands of databases across the enterprise or in the Cloud.

A brief primer about Exadata:

Oracle Exadata Database Machine is engineered to be the highest performing and most available platform for running Oracle Databases. It is a modern architecture featuring scale-out industry-standard database servers, scale-out intelligent storage servers, and an extremely high speed InfiniBand internal fabric that connects the database and storage servers. Unique software algorithms in Exadata storage software implement database intelligence in storage, PCI-based flash, and the InfiniBand network to deliver higher performance and high capacity at lower costs than other platforms. Oracle Exadata Database Machine runs all types of database workloads including Online Transaction Processing (OLTP), Data Warehousing (DW), and a consolidation of mixed workloads. This machine powers and protects the most important databases, and is the ideal foundation for a consolidated database cloud.

Oracle Exadata Database Machine includes all the hardware needed to run Oracle databases. The database servers, storage servers and network are pre-configured, pre-tuned and pretested by Oracle engineers, eliminating the weeks of effort typically required to deploy a high performance system. Extensive end-to-end testing ensures all components work together and there are no performance bottlenecks or single points of failure that can affect the complete system.

All Oracle Exadata Database Machines are configured identically so customers benefit from the experience of other users who have deployed them for their mission-critical applications. Customer machines are also identical to the machines used by Oracle Support for problem identification and resolution and by Oracle Engineering for database development. Any applications that on the Oracle database can be seamlessly migrated to Oracle Exadata Database Machine with no changes to the application.

Oracle Exadata Database Machine uses a scale-out architecture for both database servers and storage servers. As Oracle Exadata Database Machine grows, more database CPUs, storage and networking are added in a balanced fashion, ensuring scalability without bottlenecks.

2

RA Architecture

In this chapter we will go over the various hardware and software units that integrate into the one whole system called the Recovery Appliance. A good overview of clusterware, ASM & RAC is presented. The metadata database running on the RA is discussed. Finally the RA ecosystem is explored.

What powers the Recovery Appliance X6?

As we already know, the Recovery Appliance is built around the Exadata architecture. It consists of compute servers (database nodes), storage servers (cells), and the networking all integrated into one rack. The secret sauce that binds all these together into one cohesive performant unit is the storage software. Real Application Cluster (RAC) and Automatic Storage Management (ASM) are deployed for the databases. In addition for the RA we have the special ZDLRA software.

The base rack configuration consists of two compute servers and three storage servers. Up to 18 storage servers may be added to form a full rack. You can customize the configuration to accommodate your needs and add compute and storage capacity on demand. Up to 18 full racks can be connected to form a single cluster.

Each X6-2 compute server has the following components:

2x22-core Intel Xeon E5-2699 v4 processors

256GB Memory

2 x InfiniBand QDR (40 Gb/s) ports

3 x 1GbE/10GbE Ethernet ports (copper)

2 x 10GbE Ethernet SFP+ ports (optical)

1 Ethernet port for Integrated Lights Out Manager (ILOM) for remote management

2 x Redundant hot-swappable Power Supplies

2 x 16Gb Fibre Channel ports (optional)

Each X6-2L storage server has the following components:

2x10-core Intel Xeon E5-2630 v4 processors

12 x 8 TB 7200 RPM High Capacity disks

4x3.2 TB NVMe PCIe 3.0 flash cards

2 x InfiniBand QDR (40 Gb/s) ports

1 Ethernet port for ILOM for remote management

2 x Redundant hot-swappable Power Supplies

Oracle Secure Backup (OSB) tape management software is bundled with the appliance.

If you decide to use other tape solutions, you can install the client agent of a third-party media manager library, such as NetBackup or Tivoli, on the compute servers. You can then configure Recovery Appliance as a client over the 10 GbE network.

A sampling of the /etc/hosts file:

192.168.10.5 slcm03adm03-priv1 slcm03adm03-priv1.us.oracle.com

192.168.10.6 slcm03adm03-priv2 slcm03adm03-priv2.us.oracle.com

192.168.10.7 slcm03adm04-priv1 slcm03adm04-priv1.us.oracle.com

192.168.10.8 slcm03adm04-priv2 slcm03adm04-priv2.us.oracle.com

192.168.10.16 slch30celadm01-priv slch30celadm01-priv.us.oracle.com

192.168.10.17 slch30celadm02-priv slch30celadm02-priv.us.oracle.com

192.168.10.18 slch30celadm03-priv slch30celadm03-priv.us.oracle.com

Each compute node has dual IPs for the private InfiniBand interconnect.

The following software processes run on the storage cell:

- Cell Server (CELLSRV) services request for disk I/O and advanced Exadata

- Cell services, such as predicate processing offload. CELLSRV is implemented as a multi-threaded process and should be expected to use the largest portion of processor cycles on a storage cell.

- Management Server (MS) provides standalone storage cell management and configuration.

- Restart Server (RS) monitors the Cell Server and Management Server processes and restarts them, if necessary.

The Software Story:

The special ZDLRA software provides the critical functionality under the covers for the Recovery Appliance.

To determine the installed Exadata software version on the RA you may use the imageinfo command.

On the compute nodes:

[root@localhost ~]# imageinfo

..

Image version: 12.1.2.3.0

..

On the storage cells:

[root@localhost ~]# imageinfo

..

Active image version: 12.1.2.3.0

..

Let us turn our attention now on to cluster clues!

The **Grid Infrastructure (GI)** comprising of Oracle Clusterware and ASM functionality is installed on the compute nodes. Oracle Clusterware provides the infrastructure necessary to run Oracle RAC. Oracle Clusterware also manages resources, such as virtual IP (VIP) addresses, databases, listeners, services, and so on. These resources are generally named ora.entity_name.

resource_type_abbreviation, such as ora.mydb.db, which is the name of a resource that is a database.

CRSCTL is a command line utility for interfacing with the Oracle Clusterware, parsing and calling Oracle Clusterware APIs for Oracle Clusterware objects. It provides cluster-aware commands with which you can perform check, start, and stop operations on the cluster. You can run these commands from any node in the cluster. The CRSCTL commands may be used to perform several operations on Oracle Clusterware, such as starting and stopping Oracle Clusterware resources, enabling and disabling Oracle Clusterware daemons, checking the health of the cluster etc.

[oracle@localhost ~]$ /u01/app/12.1.0.2/grid/bin/crsctl query crs activeversion

Oracle Clusterware active version on the cluster is [12.1.0.2.0]

The olsnodes command provides the cluster name and the list of nodes and other information for all nodes participating in the cluster. You can use this command to quickly check that your cluster is operational, and all nodes are registered as members of the cluster. This command also provides an easy method for obtaining the node numbers.

[oracle@localhost ~]$ /u01/app/12.1.0.2/grid/bin/olsnodes -c

clustzdlra2

[oracle@localhost ~]$ /u01/app/12.1.0.2/grid/bin/olsnodes -n

slcm03adm03 1

slcm03adm04 2

We can also ascertain the status of various cluster resources using 'crs_stat -t'.

We use SRVCTL to manage cluster configuration information. You can use SRVCTL commands to add, remove, start, stop, modify, enable, and disable a number of entities, such as databases, instances, listeners, SCAN listeners, services, Grid Naming Service (GNS), and Oracle ASM.

Some SRVCTL operations modify the configuration data stored in the Oracle Cluster Registry (OCR). SRVCTL performs other operations, such as starting and stopping instances, by sending requests to the Oracle Clusterware process (CRSD), which then starts or stops the Oracle Clusterware resources.

The Oracle RDBMS software is also at 12.1.0.2.0 patch level.

All about ASM:

Oracle Automatic Storage Management (ASM) is a volume manager and a file system for Oracle Database files that supports single-instance Oracle Database and Oracle Real Application Clusters (Oracle RAC) configurations.

Oracle ASM is the Oracle's recommended storage management solution that provides an alternative to conventional volume managers, file systems, and raw devices.

Oracle ASM uses disk groups to store data files; an Oracle ASM disk group is a collection of disks that Oracle ASM manages as a unit. Within a disk group, Oracle ASM exposes a file system interface for Oracle Database files. The content of files that are stored in a disk group is evenly distributed to eliminate hot spots and to provide uniform performance across the disks. The performance is comparable to the performance of raw devices.

The Oracle ASM normal and high redundancy disk groups enable two-way and three-way mirroring respectively.

Oracle ASM has easy to use management interfaces such as SQL*Plus, the Oracle ASM Command Line Utility (ASMCMD) command-line interface.

An Oracle ASM instance has a System Global Area (SGA) and background processes that are similar to those of Oracle database instance. Oracle ASM instances mount disk groups to make Oracle ASM files available to database instances; Oracle ASM instances do not mount databases. Oracle ASM and database instances require shared access to the disks in a disk group.

A disk group consists of multiple disks and is the fundamental object that Oracle ASM manages. The disk groups are striped across all disks and Exadata storage servers to maximize I/O bandwidth and performance, and simplify management.

The Reliable Data Socket (RDS) protocol should be used over the InfiniBand network for database server to cell communication and Oracle RAC communication. Check the alert log to verify the private network for Oracle RAC is running the RDS protocol over the InfiniBand network. The following message should be in the log: cluster interconnect IPC version: Oracle RDS/IP (generic).

After Exadata storage server is configured, the database server host must be configured with the cellinit.ora and the cellip.ora files to use the cell. The files are located in the /etc/oracle/cell/network-config directory. The cellinit.ora file contains the database IP addresses. The cellip.ora file contains the storage cell IP addresses. Both files are located on the database server host.

In the Recovery Appliance, the ASM instances are clustered meaning an ASM instance runs on each compute node.

[oracle@localhost ~]$ srvctl status asm

ASM is running on slcm03adm04,slcm03adm03

The ASM binaries share the same home as the Clusterware binaries.

Please note if role separation is implemented the GI software will be owned by user like 'grid' rather than RDBMS software owner like 'oracle'.

To connect to the ASM environment we set the SID first.

[oracle@localhost ~]$. oraenv

ORACLE_SID = [zdlra21] ? +ASM1

We can now use the ASM command line utility asmcmd. To list the ASM diskgroups we can use the lsdg command.

[oracle@localhost ~]$ asmcmd

ASMCMD> lsdg

State Type Rebal Sector Block AU Total_MB Free_MB Req_mir_free_MB Usable_file_MB Offline_disks Voting_files Name

MOUNTED HIGH N 512 4096 4194304 6553600 2905888 163840 914016 0 Y **CATALOG/**

MOUNTED NORMAL N 512 4096 4194304 257753088 19052140 2684928 8183606 0 N **DELTA/**

To list the attributes of a diskgroup:

ASMCMD> lsattr -l -G CATALOG

Name Value

..

appliance._partnering_type EXADATA FIXED

appliance.mode TRUE

au_size 4194304

cell.smart_scan_capable TRUE

compatible.asm 12.1.0.2.0

compatible.rdbms 12.1.0.2.0

disk_repair_time 3.6h

..

We can also login to the ASM instance.

[oracle@localhost dbs]$ sqlplus

SQL*Plus: Release 12.1.0.2.0 Production on ..

Enter user-name: / as sysasm

Connected to:

Oracle Database 12c Enterprise Edition Release 12.1.0.2.0 - 64bit Production

With the Real Application Clusters and Automatic Storage Management options

SQL> show spparameter

SID NAME TYPE VALUE

----- ------------------- ------ -----------------------

..

* asm_diskstring string o/*/*

+ASM1 cluster_interconnects string 192.168.10.5:192.168.10.6

+ASM2 cluster_interconnects string 192.168.10.7:192.168.10.8

* memory_target big integer 0

* sga_target big integer 2G

..

As you can see automatic memory management is disabled for ASM instances.

ASM in storage cell:

Each storage cell has a physical disk. The physical disk is an actual device within the storage cell that constitutes a single disk drive spindle. Within the storage cells, a logical unit number (LUN) defines a logical storage resource from which a single cell disk can be created.

A cell disk is an Oracle Exadata Storage Server Software abstraction built on the top of a LUN. After a cell disk is created from the LUN, it is managed by Oracle Exadata Storage Server Software and can be further subdivided into grid disks, which are directly exposed to the database and Oracle ASM instances. Each grid disk is a potentially noncontiguous partition of the cell disk that is directly exposed to Oracle ASM to be used for the Oracle ASM disk group creations and expansions.

A LUN is created from a physical disk. A cell disk is created on a LUN. Multiple grid disks can be created on a cell disk. The Oracle Exadata Storage Server grid disks are specified with the following pattern:

o/cell_IPaddress/griddisk_name

The following lists the grid disks (12 per cell for each diskgroup).

ASMCMD> lsdsk

Path

o/192.168.10.16/CATALOG_CD_00_slch30celadm01

..

o/192.168.10.16/CATALOG_CD_11_slch30celadm01

o/192.168.10.16/DELTA_CD_00_slch30celadm01

..

o/192.168.10.16/DELTA_CD_11_slch30celadm01

o/192.168.10.17/CATALOG_CD_00_slch30celadm02

..

o/192.168.10.17/CATALOG_CD_11_slch30celadm02

o/192.168.10.17/DELTA_CD_00_slch30celadm02

..

o/192.168.10.17/DELTA_CD_11_slch30celadm02

o/192.168.10.18/CATALOG_CD_00_slch30celadm03

..

o/192.168.10.18/CATALOG_CD_11_slch30celadm03

o/192.168.10.18/DELTA_CD_00_slch30celadm03

..

o/192.168.10.18/DELTA_CD_11_slch30celadm03

The Oracle Cluster Registry (OCR) file is located in the ASM delta diskgroup.

The cluster voting disks are located as under:

[oracle@localhost ~]$ /u01/app/12.1.0.2/grid/bin/crsctl query css votedisk

STATE File Universal Id File Name Disk group

-- ----- ----------------- --------- ---------

1. ONLINE 92b3aeffa9144f52bf83ff7f68ee44af (o/192.168.10.16/
DELTA_CD_02_slch30celadm01) [DELTA]

2. ONLINE 007502da8d274fd0bf04edb087fc4f70 (o/192.168.10.17/
DELTA_CD_02_slch30celadm02) [DELTA]

3. ONLINE 1614fc701eba4facbf36f3d548f8833e (o/192.168.10.18/
DELTA_CD_02_slch30celadm03) [DELTA]

Located 3 voting disk(s).

Thus these are spread across 3 storage cells.

The cell alert log is located in a folder like this:

/opt/oracle/cell/log/diag/asm/cell/<hostname>/trace/alert.log

CellCLI, dcli & DBMCLI:

The CellCLI utility is the command-line administration tool for Oracle Exadata Storage Server Software. CellCLI runs on each cell to enable you to manage an individual cell.

You use CellCLI to start and stop the cell, to manage cell configuration information, to enable or disable cells, and to manage objects in the cell environment.

We login to the cell as the celladmin user and invoke CellCLI. The 'list cell detail' describes the cell configuration.

```
[celladmin@localhost ~]$ cellcli
```

CellCLI: Release 12.1.2.1.0 - Production on ..

CellCLI> list cell detail

name: slch30celadm01

..

flashCacheMode: WriteBack

..

status: online

..

upTime: 238 days, 0:31

..

cellsrvStatus: running

msStatus: running

rsStatus: running

The dcli utility facilitates centralized management across an Oracle Exadata Database Machine by automating the execution of shell and CellCLI commands on a set of compute nodes and storage cells and returning the output to the node or cell where the dcli utility is run.

The dcli utility requires Python version 2.3 or later. In addition, use of this tool assumes prior setup of SSH user-equivalence across nodes and cells. Setting user-equivalence enables you to issue commands to remote nodes/cells without having to enter the passwords.

In the example below root is the user and the mycells file lists the hostnames of 3 cells.

slch30celadm01

slch30celadm02

slch30celadm03

[root@localhost ~]# dcli -l root -g /home/oracle/mycells "cellcli -e list flashcache detail"

The DBMCLI utility is the command-line administration tool for configuring database servers, and managing objects in the server environment.

We login to the database server as the dbmadmin user and invoke DBMCLI. Just like the storage cells, we have the Management Server (MS) and Restart Server (RS) processes running on the database servers.

[dbmadmin@localhost ~]$ dbmcli

DBMCLI: Release - Production on ..

DBMCLI> list dbserver detail

name: slcm03adm03

..

interconnect1: ib0

interconnect2: ib1

..

status: online

..

upTime: 154 days, 1:52

msStatus: running

rsStatus: running

What are Real Application Cluster (RAC) databases?

Non-cluster Oracle databases have a one-to-one relationship between the Oracle database and the instance. Oracle RAC environments, however, have a one-to-many relationship between the database and instances. An Oracle RAC database can have up to 100 instances, all of which access one database. All database instances must use the same interconnect, which can also be used by Oracle Clusterware.

Oracle RAC databases differ architecturally from non-cluster Oracle databases in that each Oracle RAC database instance also has at least one additional thread of redo for each instance and an instance-specific undo tablespace. The combined processing power of the multiple servers can provide greater throughput and Oracle RAC scalability than is available from a single server.

A cluster comprises multiple interconnected computers or servers that appear as if they are one server to end users and applications. The Oracle RAC option with Oracle Database enables you to cluster Oracle databases. Oracle RAC uses Oracle Clusterware for the infrastructure to bind multiple servers so they operate as a single system.

The RA metadata database:

This houses the RMAN recovery catalog and also manages ASM storage locations for backups and redo streams from target databases. Expectedly this is a clustered database as confirmed by srvctl.

[oracle@localhost ~]$ srvctl status database -db zdlra2

Instance zdlra21 is running on node slcm03adm03

Instance zdlra22 is running on node slcm03adm04

The init parameter file in $ORACLE_HOME/dbs just has a single entry pointing to the server parameter file.

[oracle@localhost dbs]$ cat initzdlra21.ora

SPFILE='+CATALOG/zdlra2/spfilezdlra2.ora'

Let us login and check out the key instance parameters.

Make sure you set the environment variables like the Oracle SID and home correctly first.

```
[oracle@localhost dbs]$ sqlplus

SQL*Plus: Release 12.1.0.2.0 Production on ..


Enter user-name: / as sysdba

Connected to:

Oracle Database 12c Enterprise Edition Release 12.1.0.2.0 -
64bit Production

With the Partitioning, Real Application Clusters and
Automatic Storage Management options

SQL> show spparameter

..

cluster_database boolean true

..

zdlra21 cluster_interconnects string 192.168.10.5:192.168.10.6

zdlra22 cluster_interconnects string 192.168.10.7:192.168.10.8

..

* db_create_file_dest string +CATALOG

* db_create_online_log_dest_1 string +CATALOG

..

* db_recovery_file_dest string +DELTA

* db_recovery_file_dest_size big integer 4096G

..

* pga_aggregate_limit big integer 176G

..

* sga_target big integer 64G
```

The automatic memory management feature is disabled for the RDBMS instances also.

Note: This catalog is NOT housed (no pun intended!) in a container database.

DBMS_RA:

This PL/SQL package is the command-line interface to the Recovery Appliance. This package owned by the primary schema (RASYS) in the metadata database provides the underlying functionality for Enterprise Manager 12c Cloud Control plugin for the Recovery Appliance.

Key views:

A few important views belonging to RASYS user are:

ra_database

ra_db_access

ra_protection_policy

ra_storage_location

We have 27 views specific to the Recovery Appliance all prefixed with RA.

In addition we have 64 recovery catalog views.

RA SBT:

The Recovery Appliance backup module is an Oracle-supplied media management SBT library.

RMAN uses this module for transferring target database backups to the Recovery Appliance and

restoring backups from the Recovery Appliance. On the RA it is found under $ORACLE_HOME/lib as under:

/u01/app/oracle/product/12.1.0.2/dbhome_1/lib/libra.so

This module must be installed in every Oracle home of target databases that backup to the Recovery Appliance.

The Recovery Appliance backup module may be downloaded from OTN here:

http://www.oracle.com/technetwork/database/availability/oracle-zdlra-backup-module-2279224.html

The Recovery Appliance Ecosystem

So what are the key players in this space?

Figure 2-1 illustrates the various entities that make up the RA environment.

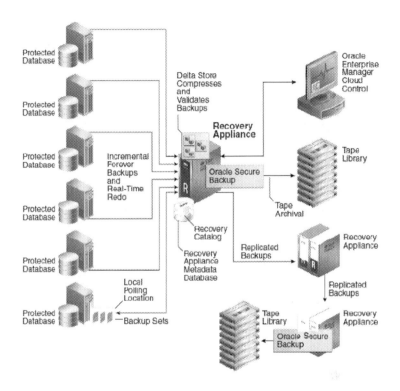

Figure 2-1 The Recovery Appliance Ecosystem

Recovery Appliance:

This is the heart of the environment which ingests backups and real-time redo streams from the target databases. The Recovery Appliance hosts the metadata database which contains the RMAN recovery catalog. This physical catalog is further provisioned into multiple virtual recovery catalogs. This database is responsible for managing storage locations for the backups.

RASYS is the RA administrator schema and owns the recovery catalog and the DBMS_RA package.

In addition the metadata database contains multiple user accounts. This user sends and receives backups for target databases and can also maintain recovery catalog metadata for these databases.

Each such user maps to a virtual private catalog owner.

Protected databases:

Target databases use the Recovery Appliance as a destination for centralized RMAN backup and recovery. These are termed protected databases. Each protected database uses the recovery catalog in the Recovery Appliance metadata database. A heterogeneous mix of protected databases can include Oracle10g, Oracle11g and Oracle12c flavors.

Oracle Secure Backup:

Oracle Secure Backup (OSB) tape management software is bundled with the appliance. The protected database hosts do not need this RMAN-integrated media management software. The Recovery Appliance automatically manages the copy of backups to tape for all protected databases.

Oracle Enterprise Manager Cloud Control (with ZDLRA plugin):

Administrators can easily manage all Recovery Appliances, protected databases, and even tape devices in the Recovery Appliance ecosystem. A Cloud Control user with the required roles and privileges is needed to manage a specific Recovery Appliance.

The RA Workflow:

The Recovery Appliance uses an 'incremental-forever' strategy.

Each protected database seeds the Recovery Appliance with the first and the only ever initial level 0 incremental backup.

Next each protected database sends a level 1 (cumulative) incremental backup to the Recovery Appliance.

On ingesting this backup the Recovery Appliance validates, compresses and indexes it, to create 'virtual' full backup. (a complete database image as of one distinct point in time)

The RA then writes the backup to a storage location.

If replication is configured, the upstream Recovery Appliance forwards the backup to the downstream Recovery Appliance.

If automated copy-to-tape policies are enabled, the Recovery Appliance archives the backup to tape.

The Recovery Appliance periodically validates backups both on disk and tape.

It also performs automated space management by deleting obsolete and expired backups, both on disk and tape, and optimizing storage locations.

The Recovery Appliance employs **real-time** redo transport feature for the protected databases. This substantially reduces the window of potential data loss that exists between successive archived redo log backups. Typical Recovery Point Objective (RPO) is zero to sub-second when this is enabled.

With real-time redo transport enabled, a protected database generates redo changes in memory, and then immediately transfers them to the Recovery Appliance, which validates them and writes them to a staging area. When the protected database performs an online redo log switch, the Recovery Appliance converts and assembles the redo changes into compressed archived redo log file backups. The Recovery Appliance catalog automatically tracks these archived redo log backups in its recovery catalog.

Just like DataGuard, the Recovery Appliance automagically performs gap resolution for archived logs. If the redo stream terminates unexpectedly, then the Recovery Appliance can close the incoming redo stream and create a partial archived redo log file backup, thereby protecting transactions up to the last change that the appliance received. When the Recovery Appliance detects that the redo stream has restarted, it automatically retrieves all missing archived redo log files from the protected database.

Since the Recovery Appliance automatically converts real-time redo into archived log backups, it is NOT necessary to back up archived logs on the database host.

Caution: Real-time redo transport is not available for Oracle10g databases.

Storage locations:

As the Recovery Appliance receives backups from protected databases, it indexes them and stores them in containers called delta pools. A delta pool is the set of data file blocks from which virtual full backups are born. Each data file has its own assigned delta pool.

The collection of all such delta pools form the delta store. All data file and archived redo log backups reside in the delta store.

The backups are validated and compressed and are stored in an ASM disk group called **DELTA**.

The datafiles of the metadata database reside in another diskgroup named **CATALOG**.

```
SQL> desc ra_storage_location

Name Null? Type

---------------------- -------- -------------------------

NAME NOT NULL VARCHAR2(128)

SL_KEY NOT NULL NUMBER

DISK_GROUPS VARCHAR2(4000)

MIN_ALLOC NUMBER

TOTAL_SPACE NUMBER

USED_SPACE NUMBER

FREESPACE NUMBER

FREESPACE_GOAL NUMBER

LAST_CHECK_FILES TIMESTAMP(6) WITH TIME ZONE

SYSTEM_PURGING_SPACE NUMBER
```

Please note the numbers are in GB.

The delta store (where backups reside) uses a new ASM file type designed just for ZDLRA called CONTAINER.

Replication:

In Recovery Appliance replication, one Recovery Appliance (the upstream RA) pushes backups to another Recovery Appliance (the downstream RA). The upstream RA, after processing the backups forwards the backups to the downstream RA. .The downstream RA processes these backups and then updates its own metadata database.

The reconciliation or syncing up of metadata between the upstream RA and the downstream RA is continuously and automagically performed.

Polling:

A polling location is a file system directory (NFS mounted), outside the Recovery Appliance, that stores backup pieces and archived redo log files for a protected database.

The Recovery Appliance polls this location at specified intervals, retrieves any new backups, and processes and stores them on the Recovery Appliance.

3

OEDA for RA

The *Oracle Exadata Deployment Assistant (OEDA)* is used to create the Recovery Appliance configuration files. These files are used with the *OneCommand* installation utility to help automate the deployment process and ensure that the Recovery Appliance is configured to your specifications.

In this chapter we will navigate the various key screens of this tool to get an understanding of the type of data that has to be input. We will also look at the software installation steps for this appliance.

Prior to running this tool, the data center has to be ready for RA installation. The site checklist may be obtained from Oracle Advanced Customer Support (ACS). Complete the following checklists to ensure the site is well prepared:

System Components

Data Center Room

Data Center Environment

Access Route

Facility Power

Safety

Logistics

Network Configuration

Auto Service Request

Replication and Tape Backup

Configuration files:

Oracle Exadata Deployment Assistant has been used to configure the Oracle Exadata Database Machine or SuperCluster. Now it has been enhanced to configure the Recovery Appliance also.

As pre-work gather all the current network settings by working with the network and database administrators.

Then identify the settings to use for the Recovery Appliance.

Validation of the generated configuration files is essential before delivery and installation of the Recovery Appliance.

Ensure the computer running the Oracle Exadata Deployment Assistant is on the same network as that of the Recovery Appliance. You may run this tool on Linux(64 bit), Solaris(64 bit), OSX (64 bit) and Windows.

Please download the latest version of OneCommand zip file from My Oracle Support note 1927416.1 or 888828.1 for your operating system.

Note: This utility gets updated on a monthly basis.

For example, patch 23032131 contains the April 2016 OEDA release.

Unzip the file as under:

unzip p23032131_121111_Linux-x86-64.zip

Locate and run either config.sh or config.cmd, depending on your operating system.

Follow the steps of the wizard and on the Generate page, click Create Files.

The generated zip file may be sent to the Oracle representative. The file will be named customer_name-rack_name.zip

Run the customer_name-rack_name-checkip.sh (or-checkip.cmd) to validate the network settings.

The Oracle Exadata Deployment Assistant generates the following files:

1. customer_name-rack_name.xml

    This contains all the settings for a completed configuration. To alter the configuration of a Recovery Appliance deployment, you can load this file, enter the changes, and regenerate the configuration files.

2. customer_name-rack_name.zip

    This contains copies of the configuration files. This will be used by an Oracle Advanced Customer Services (ACS) engineer for performing the installation. Also you may copy the file to the Recovery Appliance.

3. customer_name-rack_name-checkip.sh

    This is used to ensure the factory IP addresses are unique and deployment onto the data center network is successful.

4. customer_name-rack_name-InstallationTemplate.html

    This provides a report of all the configuration details.

5. customer_name-rack_name-platinum.csv

    This identifies the compute servers and storage servers covered by Oracle Platinum Services.

6. customer_name-rack_name-preconf_rack_n.csv

    This contains the component names and IP addresses used by the checkip script.

All host names and IP addresses must be unique.

The host names and IP addresses specified in the OEDA-generated file must be registered in Domain Name System (DNS) before the initial configuration.

In addition, all public addresses, single client access name (SCAN) addresses, and VIP addresses must be registered in DNS before installation.

Figure 3-1 presents the opening screen of this tool.

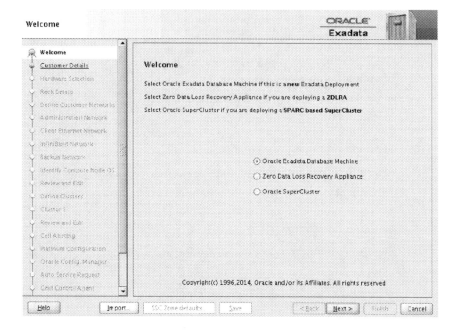

Figure 3-1 OEDA welcome page

Let us describe the various screens now.

Customer Details Page:

The key fields are below.

Network Domain Name for the RA

Name prefix: used to generate host names for all rack components. Up to 20 alphanumeric characters allowed.

Region and Time Zone: drop down list for installation

DNS: Up to three IP addresses for the Domain Name System (DNS) servers.

NTP: Up to three IP addresses for the Network Time Protocol (NTP) servers.

Hardware Selections Page:

The hardware selection page identifies the number of racks that you want to deploy at the same time, and the number of storage servers within each rack. Recovery Appliance supports a flexible configuration. You can have 3 to 18 storage servers in each rack.

Customer Networks Page:

The Recovery Appliance uses up to four networks. Each network must be on a separate subnet from the others. All addresses registered in DNS must be configured for both forward resolution and reverse resolution.

Subnet 1: The admin network provides access to the servers and switches in the Recovery Appliance, either directly or through Integrated Lights Out Manager (ILOM).

This mandatory 1 Gigabit Ethernet network connects to your existing management network. This is used for the administrative work on all components of the Recovery Appliance.

The management network connects to the servers, Oracle ILOM, and InfiniBand switches through the Cisco Ethernet switch in the rack.

Subnet 2: The ingest network connects protected database hosts to the local Recovery Appliance.

This Ethernet network must be designed to support the transfer of large volumes of data. The Recovery Appliance connects to this network using two 10 Gb connections to each of the two compute servers in the rack. You can configure the two connections as active/passive (redundant) or active/active. The compute servers support channel bonding to provide higher bandwidth and availability.

The best practice is to use LACP which supports active/active bonding using LACP(3&4).

Single Client Access Name (SCAN) supports failover between the two compute nodes in Recovery Appliance.

Please note third-party tape hardware and software also are deployed on the ingest network.

Subnet 3: The private InfiniBand network connects compute nodes and storage cells within the RA.

Oracle RAC cluster interconnect traffic also goes over this network.

Subnet 4: The replication network connects the local (upstream) Recovery Appliance to an optional, remote (downstream) Recovery Appliance.

Admin network:

You may specify starting IP address for a pool of consecutive addresses assigned to the administration network port of the compute servers, storage servers, InfiniBand switches and the ILOM port of the database and storage servers.

The pool size is calculated from the hardware selection done earlier.

The compute node names, storage cell names are all defined here along with others.

Ingest network:

You may specify starting IP address for a pool of consecutive addresses assigned to the ingest network port of the compute servers.

The pool size is calculated from the hardware selection done earlier.

VIPs and Single Client Access Name (SCAN) are defined here.

The OEDA-generated file defines the SCAN as a single name with three IP addresses on the client access network. The three SCAN addresses provide service access for clients to the Recovery Appliance. Configure DNS for round robin resolution for the SCAN name to these three SCAN addresses.

InfiniBand network:

You may specify starting IP address for a pool of consecutive addresses assigned to the administration network port of the compute servers, storage servers and InfiniBand switches.

The private names of compute nodes and storage cells are defined here.

Cluster Page:

This describes the cluster, users & groups, software locations , diskgroups, database etc.

Checking IPs:

The default factory IP address settings for the Recovery Appliance are as indicated below.

Gateway: 192.168.1.254 in all devices as required

Subnet Mask: 255.255.252.0 in all devices as required

IP Address Range: 192.168.1.1 to 192.168.1.203

How do we check for conflicts or duplicates for the above on the data center network? The checkip.sh script does exactly this job for us.

Connect the Recovery Appliance rack to the data center networks.

Log in to the system where you ran the Oracle Exadata Deployment Assistant, or to another system where you copied the generated files. The system must be on the same subnet as the Recovery Appliance. Run the checkip script, using a command like the following:

./customer_name-rack_name-checkip.sh -cf customer_name-rack_name.xml

In the preceding command, customer_name-rack_name is the name of the XML configuration file generated by the Oracle Exadata Deployment Assistant.

You must resolve all the reported conflicts and rerun the checkip script to ensure that no conflicts remain with other addresses on the network for these factory-set IPs.

ASR/Cell Alerting/OCM/Platinum Page:

For the Recovery Appliance you must configure one of the following alerting options:

- Auto Service Request (for hardware faults)

- Cell alerting (using SMTP/SNMP or both)

- Oracle Configuration Manager (Oracle support repository)

- Platinum Configuration (premium support)

Note: Oracle Platinum Services provide enhanced support at no additional cost for qualified engineered systems. This is a connected service and requires the installation of Oracle Advanced Support Gateway within the network.

It is recommended to configure Platinum for optimum operational stability.

EM Cloud Control Agent Page:

The Enterprise Manager agents are installed on the Recovery Appliance compute nodes. Specify the base folder for agent install, Oracle Management Server (OMS) hostname and the upload port.

Tape Library Page:

You can configure the tape library for the Recovery Appliance only if you use Oracle Secure Backup (OSB) as the media manager for tape backups.

Software installation:

To begin with, the RA hardware is powered on and connected to the data center network.

Then, Oracle Advanced Customer Support (ACS) will perform the software installation.

The install.sh script uses the files generated by Oracle Exadata Deployment Assistant to configure the networks, Oracle database, and other software components.

The OneCommand ZIP file that contains Oracle Exadata Deployment Assistant also contains this script. You can run this script from any system on the same network as the Recovery Appliance.

For example, the command below lists all the steps in the process.

$ ./install.sh -cf customer_name-rack_name.xml -l

The various steps/tasks performed by this script are:

1. Validate Configuration File

2. Setup Required Files

3. Create Users

4. Setup Cell Connectivity

5. Verify InfiniBand

6. Calibrate Cells

7. Create Cell Disks

8. Create Grid Disks

9. Configure Cell Alerting

10. Install Cluster Software

11. Initialize Cluster Software

12. Install Database Software

13. Relink Database with RDS

14. Create ASM Diskgroups

15. Create Databases

16. Apply Security Fixes

17. Install Exachk

18. Setup Alerting

19. Create Installation Summary

20. Resecure Machine

Certain additional configuration tasks are performed by running the ra_install perl script while logged into the compute node of the Recovery Appliance.

The various steps/tasks performed by this script are:

1. Validation and Configuration Prep

2. OS Setup

3. Oracle User Setup

4. DBFS Setup

5. Tape Backup Configuration

6. ZDLRA DB Backup Setup

7. Enable ZDLRA Services

EM Cloud Control:

For administering the entire Recovery Appliance environment, the EM management agents will be deployed on both the compute servers.

Note: MOS doc 1929507.1 has information about the plug-ins and patches required.

Once Cloud Control is configured, we are ready to start enrolling the target databases for protection by the Recovery Appliance.

4

EM for RA

EM Cloud Control (with ZDLRA plugin) provides a single pane of glass for administering the Recovery Appliance ecosystem. In this chapter we will look at a few key screens. Also the new EM Group functionality is covered.

To get to the Recovery Appliance home page login as the SYSMAN user, select Targets, then Recovery Appliances and then the name of a Recovery Appliance.

The Home page for the selected Recovery Appliance page appears.

Figure 4-1 presents the home page.

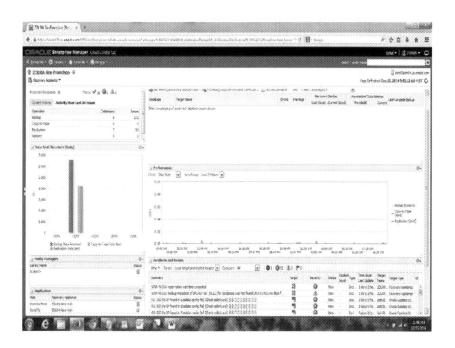

4-1 RA home page

The Recovery Appliance Home page is divided into the following sections:

Summary

This section shows the number of protected databases, and summarizes their health status, current activity, and activity within the last 24 hours. The following are clickable links:

Backup, Copy-to-Tape, Replication, and Restore.

Protected Database Issues

This section highlights any issues relating to backup and recovery status of protected databases.

Filters are available.

Data Sent/Received

This section displays daily throughput over the past week.

Performance

This section charts performance statistics for data rate and queued data.

Media Manager

This section displays the configured media manager for copy-to-tape operations.

Storage Location

This section summarizes total available space and usage of both disk recovery window goal and reserved space for all protected databases.

Replication

This section lists the downstream Recovery Appliance and the upstream Recovery Appliance.

Incidents and Events

This section summarizes all warnings or alerts of all targets associated with the Recovery Appliance.

Figure 4-2 gives the RA drop down menu below.

Figure 4-2 Main menu

Click on Storage Locations and provide the **RASYS** credential.

Storage Locations has 2 tabs : Recovery Window Space and Reserved Space

When you mouse over the name of a protected database, a message indicates the amount of storage space needed by this database to meet its recovery window, and the percentage of the total storage space required. The same is true for Reserved Space tab as well.

Figure 4-3 provides this graphic view.

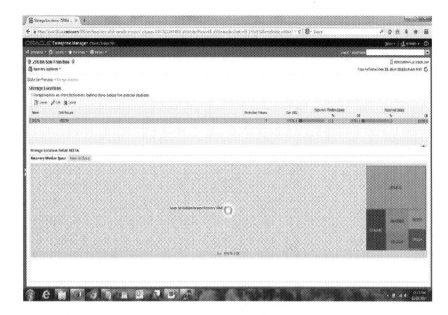

Figure 4-3 Storage Locations

Click on Protection Policies and you will see the screen below as in Figure 4-4 for example.

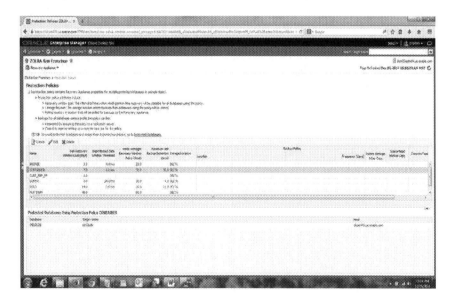

Figure 4-4 Protection Policies

Figure 4-5 lists the Protected Databases as under:

(All are clickable links)

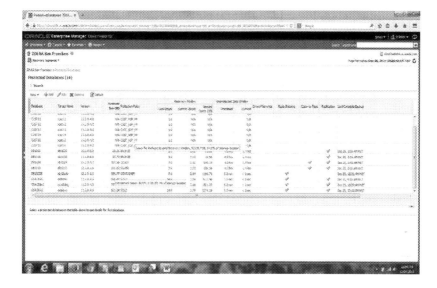

Figure 4-5 Protected Databases

Groups

Groups are an efficient and effective way to logically organize the targets in Enterprise Manager. It is a user-defined set of targets organized as a single entity. It simplifies the task of monitoring and managing the targets by allowing you to manage multiple targets from a single location. A group can include a homogenous set of targets (for example, all your production databases) or a heterogeneous set of targets (for example, all targets supporting your business application).

From the Target drop down menu, select Groups. Choose basic group.

From the Group home page, click the Create button. Give a name.

Click the Add button in the Members section, which displays a list of Targets. Search targets by using the Target Type dropdown. Select Database Instance from the dropdown list then press the Go button. All databases instance targets will be displayed; choose your databases then click the Select button. Press OK.

The group will get created.

Click the Group Name link associated with the group you just created.

The Group home page will be displayed as shown in Figure 4-6.

Figure 4-6 Group Home Page

Select Backup Configurations from the Group drop down menu.

Click Create and input name, RA name, VPC user etc. Press OK.

You will be returned to your Group's home page and a confirmation message will be displayed.

Click OK.

Select Schedule Backup from the group dropdown menu.

Accept the default settings of a Whole Database backup and to include all databases associated with the group. Click the Next button. Select backup to the Recovery Appliance and highlight your Backup Configuration.

Accept defaults and click the Next button. You can also schedule recurring backups operations on this page.

Click the Submit button. You will be returned to the group home page and will see a confirmation.

Please refer to this MOS note for prerequisites about the RA plug-in.

Note: Prerequisites for Using the Oracle Zero Data Loss Recovery Appliance Plug-in (12.1.0.1) (Doc ID 1929507.1)

EM13c with the new RA plugin may also be deployed.

5

Protection Policies

A protection policy is the central mechanism for managing database backup storage in the Recovery Appliance, based on pre-defined recovery window goals.

In this chapter we will focus primarily on policy management using the PL/SQL API (command line) method.

You can also use EM Cloud Control for GUI interface.

What does policy specify?

For every database associated with it, a protection policy specifies:

- recovery window goal for disk (RA) backups
- recovery window for tape backups
- replication or copy-to-tape of backups before deletion
- storage location (ASM diskgroup) used for backups
- backup polling policy
- maximum retention on disk before purge
- unprotected window

Every database has to belong to a policy for onboarding to the Recovery Appliance. We have 4 out-of-the-box policies: *Platinum, Gold, Silver, and Bronze.*

You can use the procedures of *DBMS_RA* package to create and manage policies.

PROCEDURE CREATE_PROTECTION_POLICY

Argument Name Type In/Out Default?

```
------------------------ -------------------- ------ --------

PROTECTION_POLICY_NAME VARCHAR2 IN

DESCRIPTION VARCHAR2 IN DEFAULT

STORAGE_LOCATION_NAME VARCHAR2 IN

POLLING_POLICY_NAME VARCHAR2 IN DEFAULT

RECOVERY_WINDOW_GOAL INTERVAL DAY TO SECOND IN

MAX_RETENTION_WINDOW INTERVAL DAY TO SECOND IN DEFAULT

RECOVERY_WINDOW_SBT INTERVAL DAY TO SECOND IN DEFAULT

UNPROTECTED_WINDOW INTERVAL DAY TO SECOND IN DEFAULT

GUARANTEED_COPY VARCHAR2 IN DEFAULT
```

We have a procedure for polling as well.

```
PROCEDURE CREATE_POLLING_POLICY

Argument Name Type In/Out Default?

------------------------------ ---------------------
-- ------ --------

POLLING_POLICY_NAME VARCHAR2 IN

POLLING_LOCATION VARCHAR2 IN

POLLING_FREQUENCY INTERVAL DAY TO SECOND IN DEFAULT

DELETE_INPUT BOOLEAN IN DEFAULT
```

Policy Management

You can use a polling policy for migrating legacy backups to the Recovery Appliance.

Connect to the RA metadata database using SQL*Plus as RASYS user.

Run the DBMS_RA.CREATE_POLLING_POLICY procedure.

In the example below, the Recovery Appliance will poll /u02/shared/ra_poll directory (NFS mounted) every 4 hours.

You want the backups deleted from this location after RA processing.

```
BEGIN
DBMS_RA.CREATE_POLLING_POLICY (
polling_policy_name => 'RA_POLL',
polling_location => '/u02/shared/ra_poll',
polling_frequency => INTERVAL '4' HOUR,
delete_input => TRUE);
END;
```

Now you may use this policy just created in our next exercise.

Connect to the RA metadata database using SQL*Plus as RASYS user.

Run the DBMS_RA.CREATE_PROTECTION_POLICY procedure.

```
BEGIN
DBMS_RA.CREATE_PROTECTION_POLICY (
protection_policy_name => 'PROD',
description => 'for tier-1 databases',
storage_location_name => 'DELTA',
recovery_window_goal => INTERVAL '31' DAY,
guaranteed_copy => 'YES',
polling_policy_name => 'RA_POLL',
max_retention_window => INTERVAL '45' DAY,
recovery_window_sbt => INTERVAL '90' DAY,
unprotected_window => INTERVAL '30' SECOND);
END;
```

Let us understand the code snippet above.

The disk recovery window goal is 31 days meaning databases must be recoverable using disk backups to any time within the last 31 days, starting from the current time.

If space pressure occurs, you want the Recovery Appliance to accept new backups after purging old backups **ONLY** after the backups have been copied to tape or replicated.

RA will purge the backups on disk after 45 days regardless of space status (hard limit).

You do want to retain backups on tape for a quarter.

This database can tolerate maximum of half a minute of data/transaction loss.

You may update a protection policy by executing the DBMS_RA. UPDATE_PROTECTION_POLICY procedure.

You can monitor policies using the Recovery Appliance catalog views.

```
SQL> desc ra_protection_policy

Name Null? Type
--------------------------------- -------- -------------------------
POLICY_NAME NOT NULL VARCHAR2(128)

DESCRIPTION VARCHAR2(128)

PROT_KEY NOT NULL NUMBER

SL_NAME NOT NULL VARCHAR2(128)

SL_KEY NOT NULL NUMBER

POLLING_NAME VARCHAR2(128)

RECOVERY_WINDOW_GOAL INTERVAL DAY(9) TO SECOND(6)

MAX_RETENTION_WINDOW INTERVAL DAY(9) TO SECOND(6)

RECOVERY_WINDOW_SBT INTERVAL DAY(9) TO SECOND(6)

UNPROTECTED_WINDOW INTERVAL DAY(9) TO SECOND(6)

GUARANTEED_COPY VARCHAR2(3)

REPLICATION_SERVER_LIST VARCHAR2(4000)


SELECT POLICY_NAME,
```

```
TO_CHAR(EXTRACT(DAY FROM RECOVERY_WINDOW_GOAL),'fm00')||':'||
TO_CHAR(EXTRACT(HOUR FROM RECOVERY_WINDOW_GOAL),'fm00')||':'||
TO_CHAR(EXTRACT(MINUTE FROM RECOVERY_WINDOW_GOAL),'fm00')||':'||
TO_CHAR(EXTRACT(SECOND FROM RECOVERY_WINDOW_GOAL),'fm00')
AS "DD:HH:MM:SS"
FROM RA_PROTECTION_POLICY
WHERE POLICY_NAME = 'PROD';
```

To delete a protection policy, execute the DBMS_RA.DELETE_PROTECTION_ POLICY procedure.

You will not be able to delete protection policies if they are associated with any protected databases.

Run this query to determine:

```
SELECT POLICY_NAME AS "removable policies"

FROM RA_PROTECTION_POLICY

WHERE POLICY_NAME NOT IN (SELECT POLICY_NAME FROM
RA_DATABASE)

ORDER BY POLICY_NAME;
```

6

Enrollment and Backup

A database that gets enrolled into the Recovery Appliance (henceforth termed protected database) will have the RA catalog as its backup metadata repository.

In this chapter we will learn about onboarding databases using the PL/SQL API (command line) method.

You can also use EM Cloud Control for GUI interface. We will also perform backups.

Steps to Enroll

1. Install the Recovery Appliance backup module.

If already not available on your database server (ra_installer.zip), you may download this from:

http://www.oracle.com/technetwork/database/availability/oracle-zdlra-backup-module-2279224.html

The Recovery Appliance backup module is an Oracle-supplied SBT library that functions as a media management library. RMAN uses the Recovery Appliance backup module to transfer backup data over the network to the Recovery Appliance. The Recovery Appliance backup module must be installed in the Oracle home of every protected database that uses RMAN to backup protected databases to the Recovery Appliance.

The Recovery Appliance backup module configuration file contains the configuration settings that are used when protected databases communicate with the Recovery Appliance. The configuration file is created automatically when the backup module is installed. This configuration file is $ORACLE_HOME/dbs/raORACLE_SID.ora by default.

In addition to installing the shared library, an Oracle wallet (cwallet.sso) is created that stores the credentials required to access the Recovery Appliance. The $ORACLE_HOME/network/admin/sqlnet.ora file is also updated to point to this location.

In the command below, prdravpc is the Recovery Appliance user owns the virtual private catalog that stores metadata for the protected database, ra-scan is the Single Client Access Name (SCAN) for the RA cluster and ra_houston is the service name of the metadata database. The library file is *libra.so*.

```
$ java -jar ra_install.jar -dbUser prdravpc -dbPass
welcome1 -host ra-scan

-port 1521 -serviceName ra_houston -walletDir $ORACLE_HOME/
dbs/ra_wallet -libDir $ORACLE_HOME/lib
```

2. Add protected database to the RA catalog.

The Recovery Appliance administrator (RASYS user) can assign the protection policy depending on recovery window goal. An estimate of space required to store backups for this protected database is also helpful.

With SQL*Plus connect to the Recovery Appliance metadata database as RASYS.

```
BEGIN

DBMS_RA.ADD_DB (

db_unique_name => 'finprd',

protection_policy_name => 'PROD',

reserved_space => '10T'); END;
```

Run this query to confirm.

```
SELECT d.DB_UNIQUE_NAME, d.POLICY_NAME

FROM RA_PROTECTION_POLICY p, RA_DATABASE d

WHERE p.policy_name=d.policy_name

ORDER BY d.DB_UNIQUE_NAME;
```

3. Grant the privileges required for performing backup and recovery operations.

The Recovery Appliance user prdravpc owns the virtual private catalog that stores metadata for the finprd database.

The protected database authenticates with this user.

With SQL*Plus connect to the Recovery Appliance metadata database as RASYS.

```
BEGIN
DBMS_RA.GRANT_DB_ACCESS (
db_unique_name => 'finprd',
username => 'prdravpc');
END;
```

Run this query to confirm.

```
SELECT d.DB_UNIQUE_NAME AS PROT_DB, d.DB_KEY, d.DBID,
d.POLICY_NAME, a.USERNAME
FROM RA_DATABASE d, RA_DB_ACCESS a
WHERE d.DB_UNIQUE_NAME = 'FINPRD'
AND a.DB_KEY = d.DB_KEY;
```

4. Register the protected database with the Recovery Appliance catalog.

```
CONNECT TARGET /
CONNECT CATALOG prdravpc/welcome1@ra-scan:1521/zdlra:dedicated

REGISTER DATABASE;
```

All these have been schematically captured below in Figure 6-1.

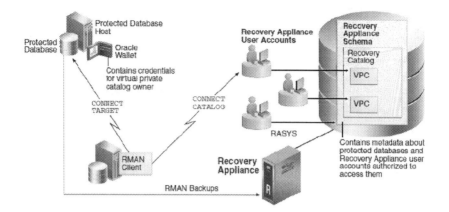

Figure 6-1 Database Enrollment

Some Do's for Protected Databases

- Use Fast Recovery Area (preferably on ASM diskgroup)

A fast recovery area is a disk location that stores backup-related files such as RMAN backups, archived redo log files, control files, online redo log file copies, flashback logs etc.. The fast recovery area automates management of backup-related files and minimizes the need to manually manage disk space for backup-related files. To use the fast recovery area as the archive destination, set the log_archive_dest parameter to USE_DB_RECOVERY_FILE_DEST.

- Use server parameter file (spfile) instead of text file(init)

- Configure controlfile autobackup on (RMAN configuration)

- Configure backup optimization on (RMAN configuration)

- Configure archived log deletion policy (RMAN configuration)

- Use Block Change Tracking file

Configuring Real-Time Redo Transport

After completing all the steps needed to enroll the protected database (outlined above) we may now implement redo transport to send streaming redo to the Recovery Appliance. The procedure is outlined below.

(All to be executed in the protected database)

1. Ensure these parameters are set as under:

REMOTE_LOGIN_PASSWORDFILE=exclusive

LOG_ARCHIVE_FORMAT='log_%d_%t_%s_%r.arc'

2. Run these statements as sysdba.

```
ALTER SYSTEM SET DB_UNIQUE_NAME=finprd SCOPE=BOTH;

ALTER SYSTEM SET LOG_ARCHIVE_CONFIG='DG_CONFIG=(zdlra,finprd)'
SCOPE=BOTH;

ALTER SYSTEM SET LOG_ARCHIVE_DEST_2='SERVICE=ra_houston
VALID_FOR=(ALL_LOGFILES, ALL_ROLES) ASYNC
DB_UNIQUE_NAME=zdlra' SCOPE=BOTH;

ALTER SYSTEM SET LOG_ARCHIVE_DEST_STATE_2='ENABLE'
SCOPE=BOTH;

ALTER SYSTEM SET REDO_TRANSPORT_USER=prdravpc SCOPE=BOTH;

SHUTDOWN IMMEDIATE;

STARTUP;
```

Test Backup to RA

Ensure the following RMAN configuration parameters are set for the protected database similar to these as under:

```
CONFIGURE BACKUP OPTIMIZATION ON;

CONFIGURE DEFAULT DEVICE TYPE TO 'SBT_TAPE';

CONFIGURE CONTROLFILE AUTOBACKUP ON;

CONFIGURE DEVICE TYPE 'SBT_TAPE' PARALLELISM 2;

CONFIGURE ARCHIVELOG DELETION POLICY TO BACKED UP 1 TIMES TO
'SBT_TAPE';

CONFIGURE CHANNEL DEVICE TYPE 'SBT_TAPE'

PARMS 'SBT_LIBRARY=/u01/app/oracle/product/12.1.0.2.0/dbhome_1/
lib/libra.so,

ENV=(RA_WALLET=location=file:/u01/app/oracle/product/12.1.0.2.0/
dbhome_1/dbs/zdlra
```

credential_alias=ra-scan:1521/zdlra:dedicated)' FORMAT '%U_%d';

CONNECT TARGET /

CONNECT CATALOG prdravpc/welcome1@ra-scan:1521/zdlra:dedicated

BACKUP TAG 'db_full_incr'

CUMULATIVE INCREMENTAL LEVEL 1

DATABASE FORMAT '%d_%U'

PLUS ARCHIVELOG FORMAT '%d_%U' NOT BACKED UP;

The above BACKUP command creates a new level 0 backup, even if one does not already exist, when it is run for the first time.

Tip: The same command may be used for scheduling the upcoming incrementals on a daily basis going forward.

If using Cloud Control we have the screen shown in Figure 6-2. You should choose the first option (RA backup).

Access the home page for the protected database and then from the Availability menu, select Backup & Recovery, and then Schedule Backup.

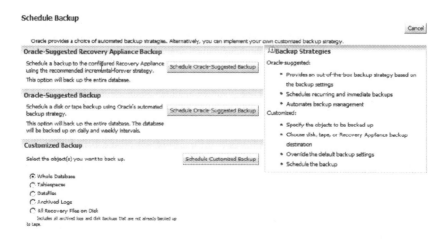

Figure 6-2 EM screen for scheduling backup

The backup reports may be viewed from the Availability menu, select Backup & Recovery, and then Backup Reports.

Test Restore from RA

How do we validate the backup just taken?

We can use a simple restore exercise without actually restoring the files. Our mantra here is:

RESTORE VALIDATE DATABASE;

RMAN identifies the backup sets and archived redo log files to be restored, and then validates them.

Tip: The database can be open with all data files online during this exercise.

CDB backup to RA (listing)

Let us review the complete listing of a container database backup below. Please take note of the strings in **bold.**

```
Recovery Manager: Release 12.1.0.2.0 - Production on Sat Feb
28 12:13:17 2015


Copyright (c) 1982, 2014, Oracle and/or its affiliates. All
rights reserved.


RMAN>

connected to target database: DB12CDB (DBID=1943136913)


RMAN>

connected to recovery catalog database


RMAN>
```

List of Backup Sets

====================

BS Key Type LV Size Device Type Elapsed Time Completion Time

------ ---- -- ---------- ---------- ------------ ----------------

79432 Incr 0 658.70M SBT_TAPE 00:00:34 28-FEB-15

BP Key: 79433 Status: AVAILABLE Compressed: YES Tag: BACKUP_DB12CDB_EXA_022815115804

Handle: VB$_1071153822_79425I Media:

List of Datafiles in backup set 79432

File LV Type Ckp SCN Ckp Time Name

---- -- ---- ---------- --------- ----

1 0 Incr 6912504 28-FEB-15 +DATA/DB12CDB/DATAFILE/ system.449.868562359

3 0 Incr 6912504 28-FEB-15 +DATA/DB12CDB/DATAFILE/ sysaux.448.868562325

4 0 Incr 6912504 28-FEB-15 +DATA/DB12CDB/DATAFILE/ undotbs1.451.868562405

6 0 Incr 6912504 28-FEB-15 +DATA/DB12CDB/DATAFILE/ users.450.868562405

BS Key Type LV Size Device Type Elapsed Time Completion Time

------ ---- -- ---------- ----------- ------------ ----------------

79439 Incr 0 292.64M SBT_TAPE 00:00:34 28-FEB-15

BP Key: 79440 Status: AVAILABLE Compressed: YES Tag: BACKUP_DB12CDB_EXA_022815115804

Handle: VB$_1071153822_79425_1 Media:

List of Datafiles in backup set 79439

File LV Type Ckp SCN Ckp Time Name

---- -- ---- ---------- --------- ----

1 0 Incr 6912504 28-FEB-15 +DATA/DB12CDB/DATAFILE/ system.449.868562359

```
BS Key Type LV Size Device Type Elapsed Time Completion Time
------- ---- -- ---------- ----------- ------------ ---------------
79443 Incr 0 361.15M SBT_TAPE 00:00:34 28-FEB-15
BP Key: 79444 Status: AVAILABLE Compressed: YES Tag:
BACKUP_DB12CDB_EXA_022815115804
Handle: VB$_1071153822_79425_3 Media:


List of Datafiles in backup set 79443
File LV Type Ckp SCN Ckp Time Name
---- -- ---- ---------- --------- ----
3 0 Incr 6912504 28-FEB-15 +DATA/DB12CDB/DATAFILE/
sysaux.448.868562325


BS Key Type LV Size Device Type Elapsed Time Completion Time
------- ---- -- ---------- ----------- ------------ ---------------
79447 Incr 0 2.61M SBT_TAPE 00:00:34 28-FEB-15
BP Key: 79448 Status: AVAILABLE Compressed: YES Tag:
BACKUP_DB12CDB_EXA_022815115804
Handle: VB$_1071153822_79425_4 Media:
List of Datafiles in backup set 79447
File LV Type Ckp SCN Ckp Time Name
---- -- ---- ---------- --------- ----
4 0 Incr 6912504 28-FEB-15 +DATA/DB12CDB/DATAFILE/
undotbs1.451.868562405


BS Key Type LV Size Device Type Elapsed Time Completion Time
------- ---- -- ---------- ----------- ------------ ---------------
79451 Incr 0 88.00K SBT_TAPE 00:00:34 28-FEB-15
BP Key: 79452 Status: AVAILABLE Compressed: YES Tag:
BACKUP_DB12CDB_EXA_022815115804
Handle: VB$_1071153822_79425_6 Media:
List of Datafiles in backup set 79451
```

File LV Type Ckp SCN Ckp Time Name

---- -- ---- ---------- --------- ----

6 0 Incr 6912504 28-FEB-15 +DATA/DB12CDB/DATAFILE/
users.450.868562405

BS Key Type LV Size Device Type Elapsed Time Completion Time

------- ---- -- ---------- ----------- ------------ ---------------

79455 Incr 1 835.41M SBT_TAPE 00:00:04 28-FEB-15

BP Key: 79456 Status: AVAILABLE Compressed: YES Tag:
BACKUP_DB12CDB_EXA_022815115804

Handle: VB$_1071153822_79430I Media:

List of Datafiles in backup set 79455

Container ID: 3, PDB Name: DB12PDB1

File LV Type Ckp SCN Ckp Time Name

---- -- ---- ---------- --------- ----

16 1 Incr 2276861 11-JAN-15 +DATA/
DB12CDB/0C44E6E4619A95B5E0531116C40AF759/DATAFILE/
soe.471.868723085

BS Key Type LV Size Device Type Elapsed Time Completion Time

------- ---- -- ---------- ---------- ------------ ---------------

79505 Incr 0 257.30M SBT_TAPE 00:00:33 28-FEB-15

BP Key: 79506 Status: AVAILABLE Compressed: YES Tag:
BACKUP_DB12CDB_EXA_022815115804

Handle: VB$_1071153822_79465I Media:

List of Datafiles in backup set 79505

Container ID: 4, PDB Name: DB12PDB2

File LV Type Ckp SCN Ckp Time Name

---- -- ---- ---------- --------- ----

12 0 Incr 6912529 28-FEB-15 +DATA/
DB12CDB/0C56237BA861F860E0531116C40A9B36/DATAFILE/
system.469.871891901

13 0 Incr 6912529 28-FEB-15 +DATA/
DB12CDB/0C56237BA861F860E0531116C40A9B36/DATAFILE/
sysaux.468.871891903

14 0 Incr 6912529 28-FEB-15 +DATA/
DB12CDB/0C56237BA861F860E0531116C40A9B36/DATAFILE/
users.467.871891905

15 0 Incr 6912529 28-FEB-15 +DATA/
DB12CDB/0C56237BA861F860E0531116C40A9B36/DATAFILE/
example.466.871891907

BS Key Type LV Size Device Type Elapsed Time Completion Time

------- ---- -- ---------- ----------- ------------ --------------

79512 Incr 0 76.98M SBT_TAPE 00:00:33 28-FEB-15

BP Key: 79513 Status: AVAILABLE Compressed: YES Tag:
BACKUP_DB12CDB_EXA_022815115804

Handle: VB$_1071153822_79465_12 Media:

List of Datafiles in backup set 79512

Container ID: 4, PDB Name: DB12PDB2

File LV Type Ckp SCN Ckp Time Name

---- -- ---- ---------- --------- ----

12 0 Incr 6912529 28-FEB-15 +DATA/
DB12CDB/0C56237BA861F860E0531116C40A9B36/DATAFILE/
system.469.871891901

BS Key Type LV Size Device Type Elapsed Time Completion Time

------ ---- -- ---------- ----------- ------------ ---------------

79516 Incr 0 147.88M SBT_TAPE 00:00:33 28-FEB-15

BP Key: 79517 Status: AVAILABLE Compressed: YES Tag:
BACKUP_DB12CDB_EXA_022815115804

Handle: VB$_1071153822_79465_13 Media:

List of Datafiles in backup set 79516

Container ID: 4, PDB Name: DB12PDB2

File LV Type Ckp SCN Ckp Time Name

---- -- ---- ---------- --------- ----

13 0 Incr 6912529 28-FEB-15 +DATA/
DB12CDB/0C56237BA861F860E0531116C40A9B36/DATAFILE/
sysaux.468.871891903

BS Key Type LV Size Device Type Elapsed Time Completion Time

------- ---- -- ---------- ----------- --------
---- ---------------

79520 Incr 0 240.00K SBT_TAPE 00:00:33 28-FEB-15

BP Key: 79521 Status: AVAILABLE Compressed: YES Tag:
BACKUP_DB12CDB_EXA_022815115804

Handle: VB$_1071153822_79465_14 Media:

List of Datafiles in backup set 79520

Container ID: 4, PDB Name: DB12PDB2

File LV Type Ckp SCN Ckp Time Name

---- -- ---- ---------- --------- ----

14 0 Incr 6912529 28-FEB-15 +DATA/
DB12CDB/0C56237BA861F860E0531116C40A9B36/DATAFILE/
users.467.871891905

BS Key Type LV Size Device Type Elapsed Time Completion Time

------- ---- -- ---------- ----------- ------------ --------------

79524 Incr 0 31.35M SBT_TAPE 00:00:33 28-FEB-15

BP Key: 79525 Status: AVAILABLE Compressed: YES Tag:
BACKUP_DB12CDB_EXA_022815115804

Handle: VB$_1071153822_79465_15 Media:

List of Datafiles in backup set 79524

Container ID: 4, PDB Name: DB12PDB2

File LV Type Ckp SCN Ckp Time Name

---- -- ---- ---------- --------- ----

15 0 Incr 6912529 28-FEB-15 +DATA/
DB12CDB/0C56237BA861F860E0531116C40A9B36/DATAFILE/
example.466.871891907

BS Key Type LV Size Device Type Elapsed Time Completion Time

------- ---- -- ---------- ----------- ------------ --------------

79529 Full 17.50M SBT_TAPE 00:00:00 28-FEB-15

BP Key: 79530 Status: AVAILABLE Compressed: NO Tag:
TAG20150228T120439

Handle: c-1943136913-20150228-00 Media: Recovery Appliance
(ZDLRA01)

SPFILE Included: Modification time: 12-FEB-15

SPFILE db_unique_name: DB12CDB

Control File Included: Ckp SCN: 6912571 Ckp time: 28-FEB-15

BS Key Type LV Size Device Type Elapsed Time Completion Time

------- ---- -- ---------- ----------- ------------ --------------

79548 Incr 0 215.02M SBT_TAPE 00:00:01 28-FEB-15

BP Key: 79549 Status: AVAILABLE Compressed: YES Tag:
BACKUP_DB12CDB_EXA_022815115804

Handle: VB$_1071153822_79479I Media:

List of Datafiles in backup set 79548

Container ID: 2, PDB Name: PDB$SEED

File LV Type Ckp SCN Ckp Time Name

---- -- ---- ---------- --------- ----

5 0 Incr 1876089 09-JAN-15 +DATA/DB12CDB/
FD9AC20F64D244D7E043B6A9E80A2F2F/DATAFILE/system.458.868562465

7 0 Incr 1876089 09-JAN-15 +DATA/DB12CDB/
FD9AC20F64D244D7E043B6A9E80A2F2F/DATAFILE/sysaux.457.868562465

BS Key Type LV Size Device Type Elapsed Time Completion Time

------- ---- -- ---------- ----------- ------------ --------------

79553 Incr 0 74.45M SBT_TAPE 00:00:01 28-FEB-15

BP Key: 79554 Status: AVAILABLE Compressed: YES Tag:
BACKUP_DB12CDB_EXA_022815115804

Handle: VB$_1071153822_79479_5 Media:

List of Datafiles in backup set 79553

Container ID: 2, PDB Name: PDB$SEED

File LV Type Ckp SCN Ckp Time Name

---- -- ---- ---------- --------- ----

5 0 Incr 1876089 09-JAN-15 +DATA/DB12CDB/
FD9AC20F64D244D7E043B6A9E80A2F2F/DATAFILE/system.458.868562465

BS Key Type LV Size Device Type Elapsed Time Completion Time

------- ---- -- --------- ----------- ------------ ---------------

79557 Incr 0 139.84M SBT_TAPE 00:00:01 28-FEB-15

BP Key: 79558 Status: AVAILABLE Compressed: YES Tag:
BACKUP_DB12CDB_EXA_022815115804

Handle: VB$_1071153822_79479_7 Media:

List of Datafiles in backup set 79557

Container ID: 2, PDB Name: PDB$SEED

File LV Type Ckp SCN Ckp Time Name

---- -- ---- ---------- --------- ----

7 0 Incr 1876089 09-JAN-15 +DATA/DB12CDB/
FD9AC20F64D244D7E043B6A9E80A2F2F/DATAFILE/sysaux.457.868562465

BS Key Type LV Size Device Type Elapsed Time Completion Time

------- ---- -- --------- ----------- ------------ --------------

79569 Incr 0 251.73M SBT_TAPE 00:00:03 28-FEB-15

BP Key: 79570 Status: AVAILABLE Compressed: YES Tag:
BACKUP_DB12CDB_EXA_022815115804

Handle: VB$_1071153822_79473I Media:

List of Datafiles in backup set 79569

Container ID: 3, PDB Name: DB12PDB1

File LV Type Ckp SCN Ckp Time Name

---- -- ---- ---------- --------- ----

8 0 Incr 2276861 11-JAN-15 +DATA/DB12CDB/
FD9BD2B44413096FE043B6A9E80ABC28/DATAFILE/system.463.868563021

9 0 Incr 2276861 11-JAN-15 +DATA/DB12CDB/
FD9BD2B44413096FE043B6A9E80ABC28/DATAFILE/sysaux.462.868563021

10 0 Incr 2276861 11-JAN-15 +DATA/DB12CDB/
FD9BD2B44413096FE043B6A9E80ABC28/DATAFILE/users.464.868563021

11 0 Incr 2276861 11-JAN-15 +DATA/DB12CDB/
FD9BD2B44413096FE043B6A9E80ABC28/DATAFILE/example.461.868563021

BS Key Type LV Size Device Type Elapsed Time Completion Time

------- ---- -- ---------- ----------- ------------ --------------

79576 Incr 0 76.60M SBT_TAPE 00:00:03 28-FEB-15

BP Key: 79577 Status: AVAILABLE Compressed: YES Tag:
BACKUP_DB12CDB_EXA_022815115804

Handle: VB$_1071153822_79473_8 Media:

List of Datafiles in backup set 79576

Container ID: 3, PDB Name: DB12PDB1

File LV Type Ckp SCN Ckp Time Name

---- -- ---- ---------- --------- ----

8 0 Incr 2276861 11-JAN-15 +DATA/DB12CDB/
FD9BD2B44413096FE043B6A9E80ABC28/DATAFILE/system.463.868563021

BS Key Type LV Size Device Type Elapsed Time Completion Time

------- ---- -- ---------- ----------- ------------ --------------

79580 Incr 0 142.84M SBT_TAPE 00:00:03 28-FEB-15

BP Key: 79581 Status: AVAILABLE Compressed: YES Tag:
BACKUP_DB12CDB_EXA_022815115804

Handle: VB$_1071153822_79473_9 Media:

List of Datafiles in backup set 79580

Container ID: 3, PDB Name: DB12PDB1

File LV Type Ckp SCN Ckp Time Name

---- -- ---- ---------- --------- ----

9 0 Incr 2276861 11-JAN-15 +DATA/DB12CDB/
FD9BD2B44413096FE043B6A9E80ABC28/DATAFILE/sysaux.462.868563021

BS Key Type LV Size Device Type Elapsed Time Completion Time

------- ---- -- ---------- ----------- ------------ --------------

79584 Incr 0 104.00K SBT_TAPE 00:00:03 28-FEB-15

BP Key: 79585 Status: AVAILABLE Compressed: YES Tag:
BACKUP_DB12CDB_EXA_022815115804

Handle: VB$_1071153822_79473_10 Media:

List of Datafiles in backup set 79584

Container ID: 3, PDB Name: DB12PDB1

File LV Type Ckp SCN Ckp Time Name

---- -- ---- ---------- --------- ----

10 0 Incr 2276861 11-JAN-15 +DATA/DB12CDB/
FD9BD2B44413096FE043B6A9E80ABC28/DATAFILE/users.464.868563021

BS Key Type LV Size Device Type Elapsed Time Completion Time

------- ---- -- ---------- ----------- ------------ --------------

79588 Incr 0 31.35M SBT_TAPE 00:00:03 28-FEB-15

BP Key: 79589 Status: AVAILABLE Compressed: YES Tag:
BACKUP_DB12CDB_EXA_022815115804

Handle: VB$_1071153822_79473_11 Media:

List of Datafiles in backup set 79588

Container ID: 3, PDB Name: DB12PDB1

File LV Type Ckp SCN Ckp Time Name

---- -- ---- ---------- --------- ----

11 0 Incr 2276861 11-JAN-15 +DATA/DB12CDB/
FD9BD2B44413096FE043B6A9E80ABC28/DATAFILE/example.461.868563021

```
BS Key Size Device Type Elapsed Time Completion Time

------- ---------- ----------- ------------ ----------------

79593 1.96G SBT_TAPE 00:00:09 28-FEB-15

BP Key: 79594 Status: AVAILABLE Compressed: NO Tag:
BACKUP_DB12CDB_EXA_022815115804

Handle: DB12CDB_1bq0demu_1_1 Media: Recovery Appliance
(ZDLRA01)


List of Archived Logs in backup set 79593

Thrd Seq Low SCN Low Time Next SCN Next Time

---- ------- ---------- --------- ---------- ---------

1 164 4115911 29-JAN-15 4140838 29-JAN-15

..

1 222 4927455 06-FEB-15 4929664 06-FEB-15


BS Key Size Device Type Elapsed Time Completion Time

------- ---------- ----------- ------------ ----------------

79655 1.95G SBT_TAPE 00:00:09 28-FEB-15

BP Key: 79656 Status: AVAILABLE Compressed: NO Tag:
BACKUP_DB12CDB_EXA_022815115804

Handle: DB12CDB_1cq0dene_1_1 Media: Recovery Appliance
(ZDLRA01)


List of Archived Logs in backup set 79655

Thrd Seq Low SCN Low Time Next SCN Next Time

---- ------- ---------- --------- ---------- ---------

1 345 6213622 20-FEB-15 6216817 20-FEB-15

..

1 404 6859782 27-FEB-15 6873566 28-FEB-15
```

```
BS Key Size Device Type Elapsed Time Completion Time

------- ---------- ----------- ------------ ----------------

79718 1.93G SBT_TAPE 00:00:08 28-FEB-15
```

BP Key: 79719 Status: AVAILABLE Compressed: NO Tag: BACKUP_DB12CDB_EXA_022815115804

Handle: DB12CDB_1dq0denu_1_1 Media: Recovery Appliance (ZDLRA01)

List of Archived Logs in backup set 79718

```
Thrd Seq Low SCN Low Time Next SCN Next Time

---- ------- ---------- --------- ---------- ---------

1 223 4929664 06-FEB-15 4937315 06-FEB-15

..

1 280 5600870 14-FEB-15 5610106 14-FEB-15
```

```
BS Key Size Device Type Elapsed Time Completion Time

------- ---------- ----------- ------------ ----------------

79779 1.77G SBT_TAPE 00:00:38 28-FEB-15
```

BP Key: 79780 Status: AVAILABLE Compressed: NO Tag: BACKUP_DB12CDB_EXA_022815115804

Handle: DB12CDB_1eq0deoe_1_1 Media: Recovery Appliance (ZDLRA01)

List of Archived Logs in backup set 79779

```
Thrd Seq Low SCN Low Time Next SCN Next Time

---- ------- ---------- --------- ---------- ---------

1 281 5610106 14-FEB-15 5625838 14-FEB-15

..

1 344 6208049 20-FEB-15 6213622 20-FEB-15
```

BS Key Size Device Type Elapsed Time Completion Time

------- ---------- ----------- ------------ ---------------

79846 97.25M SBT_TAPE 00:00:00 28-FEB-15

BP Key: 79847 Status: AVAILABLE Compressed: NO Tag:
BACKUP_DB12CDB_EXA_022815115804

Handle: DB12CDB_1fq0deps_1_1 Media: Recovery Appliance
(ZDLRA01)

List of Archived Logs in backup set 79846

Thrd Seq Low SCN Low Time Next SCN Next Time

---- ------- ---------- --------- ---------- ---------

1 405 6873566 28-FEB-15 6888325 28-FEB-15

..

1 408 6911174 28-FEB-15 6912626 28-FEB-15

BS Key Type LV Size Device Type Elapsed Time Completion Time

------- ---- -- ---------- ----------- ------------ --------------

80112 Full 18.00M SBT_TAPE 00:00:01 28-FEB-15

BP Key: 80113 Status: AVAILABLE Compressed: NO Tag:
TAG20150228T120622

Handle: c-1943136913-20150228-01 Media: Recovery Appliance
(ZDLRA01)

SPFILE Included: Modification time: 12-FEB-15

SPFILE db_unique_name: DB12CDB

Control File Included: Ckp SCN: 6912737 Ckp time: 28-FEB-15

BS Key Type LV Size Device Type Elapsed Time Completion Time

------- ---- -- ---------- ----------- ------------ --------------

80138 Full 17.75M SBT_TAPE 00:00:02 28-FEB-15

BP Key: 80139 Status: AVAILABLE Compressed: NO Tag:
BACKUP_DB12CDB_EXA_022815115804

Handle: DB12CDB_1hq0deq2_1_1 Media: Recovery Appliance
(ZDLRA01)

Control File Included: Ckp SCN: 6912787 Ckp time: 28-FEB-15

BS Key Type LV Size Device Type Elapsed Time Completion Time

------- ---- -- ---------- ----------- ------------ --------------

80155 Full 18.00M SBT_TAPE 00:00:01 28-FEB-15

BP Key: 80156 Status: AVAILABLE Compressed: NO Tag:
TAG20150228T120629

Handle: c-1943136913-20150228-02 **Media: Recovery Appliance
(ZDLRA01)**

SPFILE Included: Modification time: 12-FEB-15

SPFILE db_unique_name: DB12CDB

Control File Included: Ckp SCN: 6912802 Ckp time: 28-FEB-15

RMAN>

Recovery Manager complete.

Note: The datafile backup piece handles on the RA are always prefixed with VB$.

CDB backup to VTL (output)

You will find the actual log of a container database backup below. The backup
target is a Virtual Tape Library here.

Recovery Manager: Release 12.1.0.2.0 - Production on Sat Feb
28 12:03:11 2015

Copyright (c) 1982, 2014, Oracle and/or its affiliates. All
rights reserved.

RMAN>

connected to target database: DB12CDB (DBID=1943136913)

RMAN>

connected to recovery catalog database

RMAN>

echo set on

RMAN> set command id to 'BACKUP_DB12CDB_EXA_022815115804';

executing command: SET COMMAND ID

RMAN> backup incremental level 1 cumulative device type sbt tag 'BACKUP_DB12CDB_EXA_022815115804' database;

Starting backup at 2015-02-28 12:03:13

allocated channel: ORA_SBT_TAPE_1

channel ORA_SBT_TAPE_1: SID=514 device type=SBT_TAPE

channel ORA_SBT_TAPE_1: RA Library (ZDLRA01) SID=102C799FFA0597EDE0531116C40AF19D

no parent backup or copy of datafile 3 found

no parent backup or copy of datafile 1 found

no parent backup or copy of datafile 4 found

no parent backup or copy of datafile 6 found

no parent backup or copy of datafile 7 found

no parent backup or copy of datafile 5 found

no parent backup or copy of datafile 11 found

no parent backup or copy of datafile 9 found

no parent backup or copy of datafile 8 found

no parent backup or copy of datafile 10 found

no parent backup or copy of datafile 15 found

no parent backup or copy of datafile 13 found

no parent backup or copy of datafile 12 found

no parent backup or copy of datafile 14 found

channel ORA_SBT_TAPE_1: starting incremental level 0 datafile backup set

channel ORA_SBT_TAPE_1: specifying datafile(s) in backup set

input datafile file number=00003 name=+DATA/DB12CDB/DATAFILE/ sysaux.448.868562325

input datafile file number=00001 name=+DATA/DB12CDB/DATAFILE/ system.449.868562359

input datafile file number=00004 name=+DATA/DB12CDB/DATAFILE/ undotbs1.451.868562405

input datafile file number=00006 name=+DATA/DB12CDB/DATAFILE/ users.450.868562405

channel ORA_SBT_TAPE_1: starting piece 1 at 2015-02-28 12:03:14

channel ORA_SBT_TAPE_1: finished piece 1 at 2015-02-28 12:03:49

piece handle=DB12CDB_15q0dek2_1_1 tag=BACKUP_DB12CDB_EXA_022815115804 comment=API Version 2.0,MMS Version 3.14.10.26

channel ORA_SBT_TAPE_1: backup set complete, elapsed time: 00:00:35

channel ORA_SBT_TAPE_1: starting incremental level 1 datafile backup set

channel ORA_SBT_TAPE_1: specifying datafile(s) in backup set

input datafile file number=00016 name=+DATA/ DB12CDB/0C44E6E4619A95B5E0531116C40AF759/DATAFILE/ soe.471.868723085

channel ORA_SBT_TAPE_1: starting piece 1 at 2015-02-28 12:03:49

channel ORA_SBT_TAPE_1: finished piece 1 at 2015-02-28 12:03:56

piece handle=DB12CDB_16q0del5_1_1 tag=BACKUP_DB12CDB_EXA_022815115804 comment=API Version 2.0,MMS Version 3.14.10.26

channel ORA_SBT_TAPE_1: backup set complete, elapsed time: 00:00:07

channel ORA_SBT_TAPE_1: starting incremental level 0 datafile backup set

channel ORA_SBT_TAPE_1: specifying datafile(s) in backup set

input datafile file number=00015 name=+DATA/
DB12CDB/0C56237BA861F860E0531116C40A9B36/DATAFILE/
example.466.871891907

input datafile file number=00013 name=+DATA/
DB12CDB/0C56237BA861F860E0531116C40A9B36/DATAFILE/
sysaux.468.871891903

input datafile file number=00012 name=+DATA/
DB12CDB/0C56237BA861F860E0531116C40A9B36/DATAFILE/
system.469.871891901

input datafile file number=00014 name=+DATA/
DB12CDB/0C56237BA861F860E0531116C40A9B36/DATAFILE/
users.467.871891905

channel ORA_SBT_TAPE_1: starting piece 1 at 2015-02-28
12:03:56

channel ORA_SBT_TAPE_1: finished piece 1 at 2015-02-28 12:04:31

piece handle=DB12CDB_17q0delc_1_1
tag=BACKUP_DB12CDB_EXA_022815115804 comment=API Version
2.0,MMS Version 3.14.10.26

channel ORA_SBT_TAPE_1: backup set complete, elapsed time:
00:00:35

channel ORA_SBT_TAPE_1: starting incremental level 0 datafile
backup set

channel ORA_SBT_TAPE_1: specifying datafile(s) in backup set

input datafile file number=00011 name=+DATA/DB12CDB/
FD9BD2B44413096FE043B6A9E80ABC28/DATAFILE/example.461.868563021

input datafile file number=00009 name=+DATA/DB12CDB/
FD9BD2B44413096FE043B6A9E80ABC28/DATAFILE/sysaux.462.868563021

input datafile file number=00008 name=+DATA/DB12CDB/
FD9BD2B44413096FE043B6A9E80ABC28/DATAFILE/system.463.868563021

input datafile file number=00010 name=+DATA/DB12CDB/
FD9BD2B44413096FE043B6A9E80ABC28/DATAFILE/users.464.868563021

channel ORA_SBT_TAPE_1: starting piece 1 at 2015-02-28
12:04:31

channel ORA_SBT_TAPE_1: finished piece 1 at 2015-02-28 12:04:34

piece handle=DB12CDB_18q0demf_1_1
tag=BACKUP_DB12CDB_EXA_022815115804 comment=API Version
2.0,MMS Version 3.14.10.26

channel ORA_SBT_TAPE_1: backup set complete, elapsed time: 00:00:03

channel ORA_SBT_TAPE_1: starting incremental level 0 datafile backup set

channel ORA_SBT_TAPE_1: specifying datafile(s) in backup set

input datafile file number=00007 name=+DATA/DB12CDB/ FD9AC20F64D244D7E043B6A9E80A2F2F/DATAFILE/sysaux.457.868562465

input datafile file number=00005 name=+DATA/DB12CDB/ FD9AC20F64D244D7E043B6A9E80A2F2F/DATAFILE/system.458.868562465

channel ORA_SBT_TAPE_1: starting piece 1 at 2015-02-28 12:04:35

channel ORA_SBT_TAPE_1: finished piece 1 at 2015-02-28 12:04:38

piece handle=DB12CDB_19q0demj_1_1 tag=BACKUP_DB12CDB_EXA_022815115804 comment=API Version 2.0,MMS Version 3.14.10.26

channel ORA_SBT_TAPE_1: backup set complete, elapsed time: 00:00:03

Finished backup at 2015-02-28 12:04:38

Starting Control File and SPFILE Autobackup at 2015-02-28 12:04:38

piece handle=c-1943136913-20150228-00 comment=API Version 2.0,MMS Version 3.14.10.26

Finished Control File and SPFILE Autobackup at 2015-02-28 12:04:40

RMAN> backup device type sbt tag 'BACKUP_DB12CDB_EXA_022815115804' archivelog all not backed up;

current log archived

Starting backup at 2015-02-28 12:04:42

channel ORA_SBT_TAPE_1: starting archived log backup set

channel ORA_SBT_TAPE_1: specifying archived log(s) in backup set

```
input archived log thread=1 sequence=164 RECID=142
STAMP=870256843

..

input archived log thread=1 sequence=222 RECID=200
STAMP=870991904

channel ORA_SBT_TAPE_1: starting piece 1 at 2015-02-28
12:04:47

channel ORA_SBT_TAPE_1: finished piece 1 at 2015-02-28 12:05:02

piece handle=DB12CDB_1bq0demu_1_1
tag=BACKUP_DB12CDB_EXA_022815115804 comment=API Version
2.0,MMS Version 3.14.10.26

channel ORA_SBT_TAPE_1: backup set complete, elapsed time:
00:00:15

channel ORA_SBT_TAPE_1: starting archived log backup set

channel ORA_SBT_TAPE_1: specifying archived log(s) in
backup set

channel ORA_SBT_TAPE_1: starting archived log backup set

channel ORA_SBT_TAPE_1: specifying archived log(s) in
backup set

input archived log thread=1 sequence=223 RECID=201
STAMP=870995021

..

input archived log thread=1 sequence=280 RECID=258
STAMP=871628625

channel ORA_SBT_TAPE_1: starting piece 1 at 2015-02-28
12:05:19

channel ORA_SBT_TAPE_1: finished piece 1 at 2015-02-28 12:05:34

piece handle=DB12CDB_1dq0denu_1_1
tag=BACKUP_DB12CDB_EXA_022815115804 comment=API Version
2.0,MMS Version 3.14.10.26

channel ORA_SBT_TAPE_1: backup set complete, elapsed time:
00:00:15

Finished backup at 2015-02-28 12:06:21
```

Starting Control File and SPFILE Autobackup at 2015-02-28 12:06:21

piece handle=c-1943136913-20150228-01 comment=API Version 2.0,MMS Version 3.14.10.26

Finished Control File and SPFILE Autobackup at 2015-02-28 12:06:23

RMAN> run {

2> allocate channel ORA_SBT_TAPE_1 type 'SBT_TAPE' format '%d_%U' parms "SBT_LIBRARY=/u01/app/oracle/team01/product/12.1.0.2/dbhome_1/lib/libra.so,

ENV=(RA_WALLET='location=file:/u01/app/oracle/team01/product/12.1.0.2/dbhome_1/dbs/zdlra credential_alias=zdl1cli-scan:1521/zdlra01:dedicated')" ;

3> backup tag 'BACKUP_DB12CDB_EXA_022815115804' current controlfile; }

allocated channel: ORA_SBT_TAPE_1

channel ORA_SBT_TAPE_1: SID=514 device type=SBT_TAPE

channel ORA_SBT_TAPE_1: RA Library (ZDLRA01) SID=102C799FFA0797EDE0531116C40AF19D

Starting backup at 2015-02-28 12:06:26

including current control file in backup set

channel ORA_SBT_TAPE_1: starting piece 1 at 2015-02-28 12:06:27

channel ORA_SBT_TAPE_1: finished piece 1 at 2015-02-28 12:06:28

piece handle=DB12CDB_1hq0deq2_1_1 tag=BACKUP_DB12CDB_EXA_022815115804 comment=API Version 2.0,MMS Version 3.14.10.26

channel ORA_SBT_TAPE_1: backup set complete, elapsed time: 00:00:01

Finished backup at 2015-02-28 12:06:28

Starting Control File and SPFILE Autobackup at 2015-02-28 12:06:28

piece handle=c-1943136913-20150228-02 comment=API Version
2.0,MMS Version 3.14.10.26

Finished Control File and SPFILE Autobackup at 2015-02-28
12:06:30

RMAN> exit;

Recovery Manager complete.

7

Tape Backups with RA

We can copy the RA backups to tape using the bundled Oracle Secure Backup (**OSB**) or any other third party tape solution like NetBackup, Tivoli etc.

In this chapter we will learn about performing tape backups using the PL/SQL API (command line) method.

You can also use EM Cloud Control for GUI interface. A detailed discussion of the most popular media managers is also presented.

Benefits of RA Tape Integration

The key advantages of this tape solution are:

* Tape operations are executed by the Recovery Appliance, with no impact on the protected database host.

* It presents a flexible menu of copying weekly full and daily incremental or just daily full backups.

* OSB is pre-configured, obviating the need for third party media managers.

* Recovery Appliance has full control over tape systems and all operations are fully optimized.

* All copying to tape is automated, policy-driven, and scheduled.

Tip: Recovery Appliance copies backups to tape in the regular (non-virtual) format. If a protected database has the required media management software, then backups can also be directly restored to the database host without Recovery Appliance.

Figure 7-1 captures the Oracle recommended stack with OSB.

A Fiber Channel (FC) adapter is installed in each compute node to connect to the FC Storage Area Network (SAN).

Tape backups/restores flow **ONLY** on this network without impacting other networks.

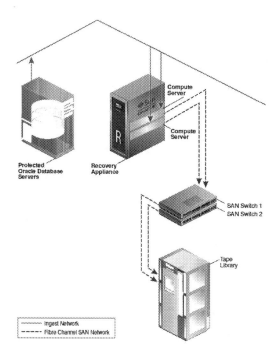

Figure 7-1 RA with Oracle Tape System

Copy to Tape Process

With SQL*Plus connect to the Recovery Appliance metadata database as the Recovery Appliance administrator.

Run these procedures:

```
1. Create a media manager library
BEGIN
DBMS_RA.CREATE_SBT_LIBRARY(
lib_name => 'osb_sbt',
```

```
drives => 12,

restore_drives => 2,

parms => 'SBT_LIBRARY=libobk.so');

END;
```

In the above example, this library can access a dozen tape drives and a couple are set aside for restores.

You may also update or delete a sbt_library.

2. Create a media manager attribute set

(Media manager libraries define parameters that apply to a set of jobs while attribute sets help further define tape backup settings for specified jobs.)

```
BEGIN

DBMS_RA.CREATE_SBT_ATTRIBUTE_SET(

lib_name => 'osb_sbt',

attribute_set_name => 'vldb',

streams => 32,

parms => 'ENV=(OB_MEDIA_FAMILY=vldb_mf)');

END;
```

We have 32 streams as the maximum concurrent connections.

We are using OSB in the example above.

Note: The parms argument has the same purpose of PARMS clause of an ALLOCATE / CONFIGURE CHANNEL command.

You may also update or delete a sbt attribute set.

3. Create a tape backup job

```
BEGIN

DBMS_RA.CREATE_SBT_JOB_TEMPLATE (
```

```
template_name => 'arch_full',

protection_policy_name => 'prod',

attribute_set_name => 'vldb',

backup_type => 'FULL,ARCH',

priority => DBMS_RA.SBT_PRIORITY_CRITICAL,

window => INTERVAL '2' HOUR);
END;
```

Backups for all protected databases assigned to the protection policy are included for copying.

The backup types available are ALL, INCR, ARCH, or FULL. The various job priorities are

SBT_PRORITY_LOW, SBT_PRIORITY_MEDIUM, SBT_PRIORITY_HIGH, SBT_PRIORITY_CRITICAL.

The two-hour window is the length of time copy tasks generated by this job can start.

Since this is an overloaded procedure, we can also use it to specify the db_unique_name of a protected database.

```
BEGIN

DBMS_RA.CREATE_SBT_JOB_TEMPLATE (

template_name => 'arch_full',

db_unique_name => 'finprd',

attribute_set_name => 'vldb',

backup_type => 'FULL,ARCH',

priority => DBMS_RA.SBT_PRIORITY_CRITICAL,

window => INTERVAL '2' HOUR);
END;
```

You may also update or delete a sbt job template.

4. Schedule the tape backup job

```
BEGIN

DBMS_SCHEDULER.CREATE_JOB(

template_name => 'arch_full',

job_type => 'PLSQL_BLOCK',

job_action => 'dbms_ra.queue_sbt_backup_task(''arch_full'')',

start_date => SYSTIMESTAMP,

enabled => TRUE,

repeat_interval => 'freq=WEEKLY; BYDAY=MON,WED,FRI;
BYHOUR=22');

END;
```

You can pause and resume the copying of backups to tape while investigating failures or performing maintenance.

When paused, in-flight copies of backups will complete and queued ones (yet to be copied) are put on hold.

```
BEGIN

DBMS_RA.PAUSE_SBT_LIBRARY(

lib_name => 'osb_sbt');
END;
```

```
BEGIN

DBMS_RA.RESUME_SBT_LIBRARY(

lib_name => 'osb_sbt');
END;
```

We can query these views for various copy-to-tape related tasks.

RA_SBT_LIBRARY

RA_SBT_ATTRIBUTE_SET

RA_EM_SBT_JOB_TEMPLATE

RA_SBT_JOB

RA_SBT_TASK

During RA installation / configuration, Oracle Secure Backup creates a media manager library named ROBOT0 with default parameters. Also default attribute sets are created. Except the library name, all the default parameters may be modified.

Tip: DBMS_RA.COPY_BACKUP procedure may be used to copy backup pieces from the Recovery Appliance to a user-specified disk or SBT destination.

For a good overview of OSB, please use the link below.

http://www.oracle.com/technetwork/database/database-technologies/secure-backup/overview/index.html

The Big 3 Media Managers

These are **Oracle Secure Backup, Symantec NetBackup for Oracle and IBM Tivoli Data Protection for Oracle.**

We will cover each one of them in some detail here.

Oracle Secure Backup

The latest OSB version is 12.1.

The Recovery Appliance compute nodes also assume the role of media servers if using the bundled OSB for copying backups to tape. The compute nodes can be connected to SAN for backups to an Oracle tape system. Also in this configuration, we will need the optional QLogic HBA card installed in each of the compute nodes.

OSB software is installed in **/usr/local/oracle/backup** folder of the compute nodes. We have a command line utility called obtool to obtain information about the configuration.

A media family is a named classification of backup volumes that share the following characteristics:

- volume ID sequence

- expiration policy

- write-allowed time period

The default settings for expiration policy and write-allowed period enable tapes to be written to indefinitely and kept forever. Volumes in a media family use either a content-managed expiration policy or time-managed expiration policy.

Content-managed volumes can only be used for RMAN operations. When you use the DELETE OBSOLETE command in RMAN to purge backup pieces, Oracle Secure Backup updates its catalog to indicate that the backup pieces are deleted, so both the RMAN repository and Oracle Secure Backup catalog are synchronized.

Oracle Secure Backup is installed with a default content-managed media family named **RMAN-DEFAULT**.

You cannot delete or rename this default media family, although you can change its attributes.

[root@localhost]# obtool

ob> lsmf

OSB-CATALOG-MF write 7 days keep 14 days

RMAN-DEFAULT content manages reuse

slcm03adm03_db write 7 days content manages reuse

slcm03adm03_fs write 7 days keep 32 days

We can configure the channel in RMAN with an OSB media family.

RMAN> CONFIGURE CHANNEL DEVICE TYPE sbt

PARMS 'ENV=(OB_MEDIA_FAMILY=vldb_mf)';

The SBT library path is the lib subdirectory under /usr/local/oracle/backup and this is linked to the library in the /lib or /usr/lib directory. The default library filename is /lib/libobk.so.

The Oracle Secure Backup SBT interface is the **ONLY** supported interface for making encrypted RMAN backups directly to tape. Also unused block compression (directly to tape) is available only with OSB.

A log of SBT operations is made on the server and typically, this sbtio.log is located in the $ORACLE_HOME/rdbms/log folder. A summary snippet is provided below.

SBT-56787 11/18/2015 10:29:08 [INFO] ------ BEGIN PERFORMANCE STATISTICS ------

SBT-56787 11/18/2015 10:29:08 [INFO] Posts : 88316 posts, 0 posts timed out;

SBT-56787 11/18/2015 10:29:08 [INFO] Waits : 11502 waits, 0 waits timed out;

SBT-56787 11/18/2015 10:29:08 [INFO] Tape Blocks Read/Written: 0/174454

SBT-56787 11/18/2015 10:29:08 [INFO] Tape Bytes Read/Written : 0/182928277504

SBT-56787 11/18/2015 10:29:08 [INFO] Messages Sent/Recv : 0/0

SBT-56787 11/18/2015 10:29:08 [INFO] SBT locks : 12819 lock contentions

SBT-56787 11/18/2015 10:29:08 [INFO] NDS locks : 1025 lock contentions

SBT-56787 11/18/2015 10:29:08 [INFO]

SBT-56787 11/18/2015 10:29:08 [INFO] Total blocks moved = 174454

SBT-56787 11/18/2015 10:29:08 [INFO] SBT buffer size = 1048576 bytes

SBT-56787 11/18/2015 10:29:08 [INFO] Tape block size = 1048576 bytes

SBT-56787 11/18/2015 10:29:08 [INFO] Total session time = 542 secs

SBT-56787 11/18/2015 10:29:08 [INFO] Time to transfer first two blocks = 15 secs

SBT-56787 11/18/2015 10:29:08 [INFO] Cumulative throughput = 321.8708 MB/sec

SBT-56787 11/18/2015 10:29:08 [INFO] Steady-State throughput = 343.4094 MB/sec

SBT-56787 11/18/2015 10:29:08 [INFO]

SBT-56787 11/18/2015 10:29:08 [INFO] ------ END PERFORMANCE STATISTICS ------

For the list of tape devices supported by OSB, please refer to

http://www.oracle.com/technetwork/database/database-technologies/secure-backup/learnmore/osb-tapedevicematrix-520156.pdf

Symantec NetBackup for Oracle

The latest Netbackup for Oracle version is 7.6.

NetBackup Server software gets installed on the following servers:

- Master server

- Media server

- Client (database) server

The NetBackup for Oracle agent software gets installed on the client (database) server.

On the database server, both the NetBackup Server software and NetBackup for Oracle agent software need to be at the same version. The software on the master server needs to be at the same or higher version compared to the database server version.

The default installation folder for NetBackup is **/usr/openv/netbackup**.

NetBackup uses its own policies (not to be confused with RA policies) to provide instructions on how and when to execute the backups. Please note these:

- An RMAN job must be associated with at least one policy in order for it to execute.

- A default policy is provided with the agent software.

- Multiple policies can be created for a single database server.

The Policy Configuration Wizard of NetBackup Administration Console provides a nice and easy interface for configuring policies with these:

- Attributes

- Schedule

- Clients

- Backup selection

The best values for most configurations are automatically chosen.

These are the key environment variables used by NetBackup for Oracle:

- NB_ORA_SERV (name of the NetBackup server)

- NB_ORA_POLICY (name of the defined Oracle policy)

- NB_ORA_CLIENT (name of the NetBackup client hosting the target database)

- NB_ORA_SCHED (name of the defined Oracle schedule)

We need to link the NetBackup library into Oracle for use with RMAN.

Shut down all Oracle databases for a given Oracle home.

cd $ORACLE_HOME/lib

ln -s /usr/openv/netbackup/bin/libobk.so64 libobk.so

Now we can configure the channel and format.

```
RMAN> CONFIGURE CHANNEL DEVICE TYPE 'SBT_TAPE' PARMS

'ENV=(NB_ORA_SERV=<storage_server>,
NB_ORA_POLICY=<policy_name>)';


RMAN> CONFIGURE DEVICE TYPE 'SBT_TAPE' FORMAT 'db_%d%U%t';
```

RA Implementation for NetBackup

NetBackup setup consists of installing NetBackup client software on each RAC node in the Recovery Appliance, having the correct network, and installing the NetBackup Master Server for Oracle RAC. The Recovery Appliance should be configured like any other Oracle RAC database in the NetBackup environment.

Use VIP names as the client names for database backups to ensure Oracle database backups are not co-mingled with regular file system backups.

Set NB_ORA_SERV to name of the interface on the NetBackup Master Server for the backup traffic.

Caution: Do NOT specify NB_ORA_CLIENT as this will restrict backups to a single RA compute node.

With SQL*Plus connect to the Recovery Appliance metadata database as the Recovery Appliance administrator.

Run these procedures:

```
BEGIN

DBMS_RA.CREATE_SBT_LIBRARY(

LIB_NAME => 'NBU_SBT',

DRIVES => 2,

RESTORE_DRIVES => 1,

PARMS =>

'SBT_LIBRARY=/usr/openv/netbackup/bin/libobk.so64');


DBMS_RA.CREATE_SBT_ATTRIBUTE_SET(

ATTRIBUTE_SET_NAME => 'NBU_DRIVE_COUNT_1',

LIB_NAME => 'NBU_SBT',

STREAMS => 1,

PARMS =>

'ENV=(NB_ORA_POLICY=dbPolicy,NB_ORA_SERV=master-10g)');


DBMS_RA.CREATE_SBT_ATTRIBUTE_SET(

ATTRIBUTE_SET_NAME => 'NBU_DRIVE_COUNT_2',

LIB_NAME => 'NBU_SBT',

STREAMS => 2,

PARMS =>

'ENV=(NB_ORA_POLICY=dbPolicy,NB_ORA_SERV=master-10g)');


DBMS_RA.CREATE_SBT_JOB_TEMPLATE(

TEMPLATE_NAME => 'nbu_prd',

DB_UNIQUE_NAME => 'finprd',

ATTRIBUTE_SET_NAME => 'NBU_DRIVE_COUNT_2',
```

```
BACKUP_TYPE  =>  'FULL,ARCH',

PRIORITY  =>  DBMS_RA.SBT_PRIORITY_HIGH);

END;
```

The job can be queued manually or through Enterprise Manager.

```
BEGIN

DBMS_RA_QUEUE_SBT_BACKUP_TASK (

TEMPLATE_NAME  =>  'nbu_prd');

END;
```

Troubleshooting

Use the following command to query the master server from the client server to verify communications:

/usr/openv/netbackup/bin/bpclntcmd -pn

Verify the NetBackup communication daemons are listening for requests:

netstat -a |grep bpcd

netstat -a |grep vnetd

Make all of the /usr/openv/netbackup/logs directories and subdirectories readable and writeable by all users (777 permissions). To enable logging on the database server (client), modify the /usr/openv/netbackup/bp.conf file with this line:

VERBOSE = #

is an integral value starting from 1 to indicate the level of logging. While the default value of 0 is sufficient you can also set the debugging level to 1, 2, 3, 4, or 5. Level 5 provides the most detailed logging.

You will find a client log /usr/openv/netbackup/logs/dbclient/log.mmddyy also available for debugging.

A NetBackup for Oracle user can create an Oracle client bp.conf file in the Oracle user's home directory on the NetBackup for Oracle client host. When a NetBackup for Oracle operation is started, the user's bp.conf file is searched before the master configuration file (/usr/openv/netbackup/bp.conf) on the client. Any option found at the user level overrides the same option's setting at the master level.

The various logs are:

On database server (client): bpdbsbora, dbclient, bphdb and bpcd

(example: /usr/openv/netbackup/logs/bphdb)

On the NetBackup master server: bprd and bpdbm

Netbackup provides the bplist command to browse Oracle backups. The command returns a list of backup file names. You should be logged into either the master server or to the client as root to run bplist.

In this example bplist searches all the Oracle backups for a client named veritas:

/usr/openv/netbackup/bin/bplist -C veritas -t 4 -R

While the -t 4 switch denotes the Oracle backups we use the -R argument to indicate the default number (999) of directory levels to search recursively.

IBM Tivoli Data Protection for Oracle

The latest version of Tivoli Data Protection for Oracle is 7.1.

Data Protection for Oracle interfaces with RMAN to send backups of Oracle databases to the Tivoli Storage Manager server.

The default installation folders are:

Data Protection for Oracle Linux /opt/tivoli/tsm/client/oracle/bin64

Data Protection for Oracle Utilities /opt/tivoli/tsm/client/oracle/bin64

Data Protection for Oracle Messages /opt/tivoli/tsm/client/oracle/bin64

Tivoli Storage Manager API /opt/tivoli/tsm/client/api/bin64

After the installation, perform these tasks.

1. Register the node with the TSM server using the TSM console.

```
tsm> REG NODE hostname password maxnummp=n
```

Here hostname is the name of this node, password is the password for this node and n is the number of channels planned for use.

2. Update the /opt/tivoli/tsm/client/oracle/bin64/tdpo.opt file with these 2 entries.

*DSMI_ORC_CONFIG /opt/tivoli/tsm/client/oracle/bin64/dsm.opt

*DSMI_LOG /opt/tivoli/tsm/client/oracle/bin64

3. Update dsm.sys file

$ cd /opt/tivoli/tsm/client/api/bin64

$ ln −s /opt/tivoli/tsm/client/ba/bin/dsm.sys .

Edit the dsm.sys file to include another server stanza with the following options:

SErvername <TSM host>

COMMMethod TCPip

TCPServeraddress <IP>

PASSWORDAccess generate

nodename <TDPONodeName>

4. Create the /opt/tivoli/tsm/client/oracle/bin64/dsm.opt file with one entry.

SErvername <TSM host>

5. Enable deletion of backups on TSM server.

tsm> update node <nodename> backdelete=yes

tsm> update copygroup standard verdeleted=0

6. Generate password file as root user.

cd /opt/tivoli/tsm/client/oracle/bin64

tdpoconf password

7. Link TDP into Oracle.

$ ln /opt/tivoli/tsm/client/oracle/bin64/libobk.so $ORACLE_HOME/lib/libobk.so

8. Test the library.

$ $ORACLE_HOME/bin/sbttest tdpo_check –libname /opt/tivoli/tsm/client/oracle/bin64/libobk.so

Here, tdpo_check is the log file name created by this program.

The only environment variable Data Protection for Oracle recognizes in an RMAN script is the fully qualified path name to the **tdpo.opt** file.

Caution: The TDPO_OPTFILE variable must be specified in uppercase characters only.

We can allocate channel as under:

RMAN>run

```
{ allocate channel t1 type 'sbt_tape' parms
'ENV=(TDPO_OPTFILE=/opt/tivoli/tsm/client/oracle/bin64/
tdpo.opt)';
backup database; }
```

TSM Catalog Maintenance

When you issue the tdposync query command, information about a backup object is displayed. Information is listed including the size and date of the backup, and whether the object is compressed, encrypted, or deduplicated by the Tivoli Storage Manager during the backup operation. You are prompted to enter date range for the query. The screen output displays information about the objects that were backed up to the Tivoli Storage Manager server between the start and end dates that you specified.

Synchronize the RMAN catalog with TSM catalog by using tdposync. This utility is used to delete Oracle backups that are stored on the Tivoli Storage Manager. It checks for items on the Tivoli Storage Manager server but not in the RMAN catalog. With this utility, you can repair these discrepancies by removing unwanted objects from the Tivoli Storage Manager and reclaim space on the server.

When you start tdposync, the following processing takes place:

1. Prompts you for the RMAN catalog owner name, password, and connect string.

2. Gathers information for the Oracle servers.

3. Queries the RMAN catalog and the Tivoli Storage Manager server.

4. Displays a list of files that exist on the Tivoli Storage Manager server but not in the RMAN catalog.

5. Prompts you to delete them.

A date range may also be given to narrow the list of files.

Caution: This deletion process is irreversible.

You may also use the tdpoconf showenvironment command to display TSM environment information.

Errors

Messages with prefix ANU are issued by IBM Tivoli Storage Manager for Databases, Data Protection for Oracle.

The messages consist of the following elements: ANU, a number and a one-letter severity code.

S Severe The product or a product function cannot continue. User response is required.

E Error An error is encountered during processing. Processing might stop. User response might be required.

W Warning Processing continues, but problems might occur later as a result of the warning.

I Information Processing continues. User response is not necessary.

Example: ANU0003S An internal processing error has occurred.

In the event of a media manager issue, RMAN always signals the ORA-19511 error.

RMAN will display the error passed back to it by the media manager. You may have to contact the media management vendor to resolve such issues. Look at the example below.

RMAN-00571: ===

RMAN-00569: =============== ERROR MESSAGE STACK FOLLOWS ======

RMAN-00571: ===

RMAN-03009: failure of backup command on t1 channel at 08/04/2006 13:18:19

ORA-19506: failed to create sequential file, name="07d36ecp_1_1", parms=""

ORA-27007: failed to open file

SVR4 Error: 2: No such file or directory

Additional information: 7005

Additional information: 1

ORA-19511: Error received from media manager layer, error text:

SBT error = 7005, errno = 2, sbtopen: system error

The simplest way to confirm the proper configuration of the media manager & RMAN integration is to allocate a channel and backup controlfile. If RMAN does not report any error then we can determine the media manager is correctly configured to work with RMAN.

Caution: With third party tape systems, the RA backups to tape SHARE the 10Gb ingest network.

8

Replication

We can copy the backups from one RA to another using replication.

In this chapter we will learn about performing replication of backups using the PL/SQL API (command line) method.

You can also use EM Cloud Control for GUI interface.

In a replicated RA configuration you can also offload tape archival to the replicated Recovery Appliance (downstream), resulting in less consumption of resources on the primary Recovery Appliance (upstream). All databases associated with a protection policy may be replicated. Once properly implemented, replication is automagically performed going forward.

Tip: The downstream RA can have different retention of backups from the upstream RA.

The metadata between the upstream Recovery Appliance and the downstream Recovery Appliance is continuously reconciled and synchronized.

Backups on any downstream Recovery Appliances can be retrieved and restored by the upstream Recovery Appliance if called upon. Also, backups may be directly restored from a downstream Recovery Appliance.

Please note archived log backups are replicated (not real-time redo) to the downstream appliance.

Implementing Replication

We have 3 distinct phases while setting up replication.

Configure Downstream RA

1. Create VPC user

2. Create protection policy

3. Create replication user

4. Add databases to policy

5. Grant access

The users may be created with just 'create session' privilege.

You have to execute DBMS_RA.GRANT_DB_ACCESS procedure to grant protected database access to both the

VPC user **AND** replication user.

Configure Upstream RA

1. Create VPC user

2. Create protection policy

3. Add databases to policy

4. Grant access

5. Create wallet

6. Create replication server

7. Add replication server to policy

The credentials for the user on the downstream RA are stored in the Oracle wallet of the upstream RA.

We use the mkstore utility.

$ mkstore -wrl /home/oracle/wallet -createALO

This creates a file named cwallet.sso in the above location.

Now we add the credentials to this wallet.

zdlra_dsnyc is the Net service name of downstream RA, ussfo_dsnyc is the replication user and welcome1 is the password for this user.

```
$ mkstore -wrl /home/oracle/wallet -createCredential \

"zdlra_dsnyc" "ussfo_dsnyc" "welcome1"
```

To confirm, you can list the credential.

```
$ mkstore -wrl /home/oracle/wallet -listCredential
```

With SQL*Plus connect to the upstream Recovery Appliance metadata database as RASYS.

Execute these procedures.

```
BEGIN

DBMS_RA.CREATE_REPLICATION_SERVER (

replication_server_name => 'from_ussfo_to_dsnyc',

sbt_so_name => '/u01/app/oracle/product/12.1.0.2/dbhome_1/lib/libra.so',

catalog_user_name => 'ussfo_dsnyc',

wallet_alias => 'zdlra_dsnyc',

wallet_path => 'file:/home/oracle/wallet');

END;
```

The server name configuration above can be arbitrary.

```
BEGIN

DBMS_RA.ADD_REPLICATION_SERVER (

replication_server_name => 'from_ussfo_to_dsnyc',

protection_policy_name => 'prod');

END;
```

> Caution: Do NOT have the same catalog database name for Upstream RA and downstream RA.

Configure protected databases

1. Add VPC credentials to wallet on upstream RA

    (and optionally on downstream RA as well)

2. Register databases in upstream catalog

3. Back up databases

Now we are ready to validate our configuration.

We can list the backup sets to ensure we have 2 copies of each set in our uni-directional replication.

Connect to both target and catalog.

RMAN> list backupset;

..

..

Backup Set Copy #1 of backup set 54321

..

List of Backup Pieces for backup set 54321 Copy #1

BP Key Status Media

------- --- ----------- ----------------------- ----------

55322 AVAILABLE Recovery Appliance (ZDLRA **San Francisco**)

Backup Set Copy #2 of backup set 54321

..

List of Backup Pieces for backup set 54321 Copy #2

BP Key Status Media

------- --- ----------- ----------------------- ----------

55322 AVAILABLE Recovery Appliance (ZDLRA **New York**)

Also we can query the RA_REPLICATION_SERVER view which describes the downstream Recovery Appliance(s) this particular Recovery Appliance replicates to.

```
SQL> desc ra_replication_server
Name Null? Type
----------------------------------- -------- -----------------------
REPLICATION_SERVER_NAME NOT NULL VARCHAR2(128)
REPLICATION_SERVER_STATE VARCHAR2(21)
PROTECTION_POLICY VARCHAR2(128)
REP_SERVER_CONNECT_NAME NOT NULL VARCHAR2(128)
PROXY_HTTP_ADDRESS VARCHAR2(519)
PROXY_TIMEOUT NUMBER
SBT_LIBRARY_NAME NOT NULL VARCHAR2(128)
SBT_LIBRARY_PARMS VARCHAR2(1024)
ATTRIBUTE_NAME NOT NULL VARCHAR2(128)
ATTRIBUTE_PARMS VARCHAR2(1024)
WALLET_PATH VARCHAR2(512)
WALLET_ALIAS NOT NULL VARCHAR2(512)
SERVER_HOST NOT NULL CLOB
```

9

Monitoring

In this chapter we will learn about various monitoring techniques available for the Recovery Appliance.

We essentially have 4 methods to monitor the RA ecosystem.

ASR

Auto Service Request (ASR) automagically opens service requests for hardware faults. These include server components like disks, fans, power supplies etc.

This is normally set up during RA installation.

EM Cloud Control (with zdlra plugin)

We have 2 important sections in the RA home page:

1. Protected Database Issues

This section summarizes the backup status for protected databases. Filters are available to narrow down the scope.

2. Incidents and Events

Incidents and events are reported for the Recovery Appliance and its targets. Filters are available here too. Since incidents are clickable links you can drill down to view detailed information.

We can also edit various metrics available out of the box.

From the Recovery Appliance menu, click Monitoring, and then click Metric and Collection settings.

Ensure 'All metrics' is selected in the View menu. Expand desired metrics and edit values as needed.

(A pencil icon in the Edit column means settings are modifiable.)

RA views

The following key views may also be queried after connecting to metadata database as user RASYS.

RA_ACTIVE_SESSION

RA_CONFIG

RA_DATABASE_STORAGE_USAGE

RA_INCIDENT_LOG

```
SQL> desc RA_INCIDENT_LOG

Name Null? Type

----------------------------------------- ----
---- ----------------------------

INCIDENT_ID NUMBER

ERROR_CODE NUMBER

PARAMETER VARCHAR2(1000)

ERROR_TEXT VARCHAR2(4000)

SL_KEY NUMBER

SL_NAME VARCHAR2(128)

DB_KEY NUMBER

DB_UNIQUE_NAME VARCHAR2(30)

TASK_ID NUMBER

STATUS VARCHAR2(6)

COMPONENT VARCHAR2(30)

SEVERITY VARCHAR2(47)

FIRST_SEEN NOT NULL TIMESTAMP(6) WITH TIME ZONE

LAST_SEEN NOT NULL TIMESTAMP(6) WITH TIME ZONE
```

SEEN_COUNT NOT NULL NUMBER

(status of incident could be one of ACTIVE, FIXED, or RESET)

RA_INCOMING_BACKUP_PIECES

RA_PURGING_QUEUE

(order of deletion of oldest backups)

SQL> desc RA_PURGING_QUEUE

Name Null? Type

```
------------------------------------------- ----
---- ----------------------------
```

SL_NAME NOT NULL VARCHAR2(128)

SL_KEY NUMBER

DB_UNIQUE_NAME VARCHAR2(30)

DB_KEY NOT NULL NUMBER

PURGE_ORDER NUMBER

NEW_RECOVERY_WINDOW INTERVAL DAY(9) TO SECOND(6)

NEW_PCT_RECOVERY NUMBER

PCT_STORAGE NUMBER

RA_RESTORE_RANGE

RA_SERVER

RA_STORAGE_HISTOGRAM

RA_TASK

SQL> desc ra_task

Name Null? Type

```
------------------------------------------- ----
---- ----------------------------
```

TASK_ID NUMBER

TASK_TYPE VARCHAR2(30)

PRIORITY NUMBER

STATE VARCHAR2(13)

WAITING_ON NUMBER

CREATION_TIME TIMESTAMP(6) WITH TIME ZONE

COMPLETION_TIME TIMESTAMP(6) WITH TIME ZONE

ELAPSED_SECONDS NUMBER

ERROR_COUNT NUMBER

INTERRUPT_COUNT NUMBER

LAST_INTERRUPT_TIME TIMESTAMP(6) WITH TIME ZONE

EXECUTE_INSTANCE_ID NUMBER

LAST_EXECUTE_TIME TIMESTAMP(6) WITH TIME ZONE

DB_UNIQUE_NAME VARCHAR2(30)

DB_KEY NUMBER

SL_NAME VARCHAR2(128)

SL_KEY NUMBER

OSPID VARCHAR2(128)

INSTANCE_ID NUMBER

ARCHIVED CHAR(1)

(processing state of task could be one of EXECUTABLE, RUNNING, COMPLETED, TASK_WAIT, FAILED etc)

Note: RA error messages occur between ranges ORA-454100 and ORA-45299 & ORA-64700 and up.

Platinum Support

This is a free service from Oracle and customers on Premium Support are entitled to this for Engineered Systems if they qualify based on certain version and patch levels. This is also normally set up during RA installation. Remote monitoring and patching are provided under this service.

Please check the link below for updates to certified platinum configuration.

http://www.oracle.com/us/support/library/certified-platinum-configs-1652888.pdf

For the Recovery Appliance, the requirements are as under:

GI & RDBMS 12.1.0.2 Jul 2015 (Quarterly Full Stack Download Patch) or later

Exadata Storage Server 12.1.2.1.2 or later

10

Reporting

In this chapter we will learn about various RA reports available to us for analysis.

Through BI Publisher, Recovery Appliance provides pre-created reports.

Access the Recovery Appliance Home page and from the Enterprise menu, select Reports, and then BI Publisher Enterprise Reports. Scroll down to the Recovery Appliance Reports subfolder. You will find links to pre-created reports listed here. The following 3 reports are critical for our review.

Capacity Planning Summary

This report captures storage growth for the Recovery Appliance. The summary table provides an instant handle on the number of days before capacity is exhausted.

Please note within this duration the Recovery Appliance will either purge backups or reject incoming backups, depending on the protection policy settings.

Data is available over a period of 7 days, 31 days and 365 days for historical trend analysis. It is graphed as well.

The network capacity planning summary provides a view of aggregated (across both RA compute nodes) network traffic over various time periods. This view shows both average and maximum rates for receive and transmit.

Data is available over a period of 24 hours, 7 days, 31 days and 365 days for historical trend analysis and is graphed.

Recovery Window Summary

This report lists protected databases not meeting their recovery window goal OR are exceeding their unprotected window threshold. Tables are also provided for details about these databases.

Figure 10-1 below captures this across protection policies.

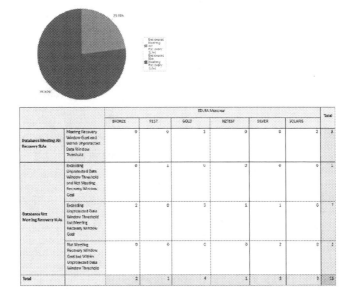

Figure 10-1 Recovery Window Summary

Top 10 Protected Databases by Data Transfer

This report ranks the top 10 protected databases measuring the amount of backup data transferred to or from the Recovery Appliance. This is computed along three factors:

- Backup data sent to the Recovery Appliance

- Replication data sent from the Recovery Appliance

- Copy-to-tape data sent from the Recovery Appliance

Data is available over a period of 24 hours and 7 days for historical trend analysis and is graphed.

Configure BI Publisher Report Jobs

You can configure BI Publisher to generate reports automagically on a regular schedule and send them by email to the database backup team.

Let us assume you are already on the Recovery Window Summary Report.

Navigate to BI Publisher Home page (by clicking Home button on right top corner), select Report Job from Create region.

You are presented with 4 tabs.

General: this has the report name.

Output: choose destination type as email and fill out relevant fields.

You can choose the format by clicking on blue button drop down list box (lower right corner).

Tip: Available report formats are PDF, HTML, RTF, Excel and PowerPoint.

Schedule: this can be used for recurring job runs.

You want to have the recovery report emailed on a daily basis. Choose Daily and for Every field input 1.

For Start field, use the date selector to enter the date and time. This job will be executed daily at the selected time.

Notification: to notify the job has finished processing, check email, specify email address and check these 4 status conditions below.

Report completed

Report completed with warnings

Report failed

Report skipped

Click Submit when done editing all the above tabs.

11

Restore and Recovery

A database backup is valid only if it can be successfully restored and recovered as needed.

In this chapter we will learn about a few advanced restore/recovery scenarios using the PL/SQL API (command line) method. You can also use EM Cloud Control for GUI interface.

PDB Recovery

First, we simulate the loss of a pluggable database within the container.

Delete all datafiles of this database from within ASMCMD.

```
ASMCMD> pwd
+data/DB12CDB/0C56237BA861F860E0531116C40A9B36/DATAFILE
ASMCMD> ls -l
Type Redund Striped Time Sys Name
DATAFILE MIRROR COARSE FEB 17 08:00:00 Y EXAMPLE.469.868637093
DATAFILE MIRROR COARSE FEB 17 08:00:00 Y SYSAUX.467.868637091
DATAFILE MIRROR COARSE FEB 17 08:00:00 Y SYSTEM.466.868637091
DATAFILE MIRROR COARSE FEB 17 08:00:00 Y USERS.468.868637093

ASMCMD> rm *
You may delete multiple files and/or directories.
Are you sure? (y/n) y
```

```
ASMCMD> ls -l
```

```
ASMCMD-8002: entry 'DATAFILE' does not exist in directory
'+data/DB12CDB/0C56237BA861F860E0531116C40A9B36/
```

Confirm deletion by trying to open this database after connecting as root to CDB.

```
SQL> alter pluggable database db12pdb2 open;
```

```
alter pluggable database db12pdb2 open
```

```
*
```

```
ERROR at line 1:
```

```
ORA-01157: cannot identify/lock data file 15 - see DBWR trace
file
```

```
ORA-01110: data file 15:
```

```
'+DATA/DB12CDB/0C56237BA861F860E0531116C40A9B36/DATAFILE/
example.469.868637093'
```

Now we can restore and recover this database from the RA backup.

```
Recovery Manager: Release 12.1.0.2.0 - Production on Tue Feb
17 08:11:30 2015
```

```
Copyright (c) 1982, 2014, Oracle and/or its affiliates. All
rights reserved.
```

```
RMAN>
```

```
connected to target database: DB12CDB (DBID=1943136913)
```

```
RMAN>
```

```
connected to recovery catalog database
```

```
RMAN>
```

```
echo set on
```

RMAN> run {

2> restore pluggable database 'DB12PDB2';

3> recover pluggable database 'DB12PDB2'; }

Starting restore at 2015-02-17 08:11:31

starting full resync of recovery catalog

full resync complete

allocated channel: ORA_DISK_1

channel ORA_DISK_1: SID=473 device type=DISK

allocated channel: ORA_SBT_TAPE_1

channel ORA_SBT_TAPE_1: SID=435 device type=SBT_TAPE

channel ORA_SBT_TAPE_1: RA Library (ZDLRA01)
SID=0F4BF4EA7E4476D9E0531116C40A1AB4

channel ORA_SBT_TAPE_1: starting datafile backup set restore

channel ORA_SBT_TAPE_1: specifying datafile(s) to restore from
backup set

channel ORA_SBT_TAPE_1: restoring datafile 00012 to
+DATA/DB12CDB/0C56237BA861F860E0531116C40A9B36/DATAFILE/
system.466.868637091

channel ORA_SBT_TAPE_1: reading from backup piece
VB$_1071153822_57811_12

channel ORA_SBT_TAPE_1: piece handle=VB$_1071153822_57811_12
tag=BACKUP_DB12CDB_EXA_021715065526

channel ORA_SBT_TAPE_1: restored backup piece 1

channel ORA_SBT_TAPE_1: restore complete, elapsed time:
00:00:01

channel ORA_SBT_TAPE_1: starting datafile backup set restore

channel ORA_SBT_TAPE_1: specifying datafile(s) to restore from
backup set

channel ORA_SBT_TAPE_1: restoring datafile 00013 to
+DATA/DB12CDB/0C56237BA861F860E0531116C40A9B36/DATAFILE/
sysaux.467.868637091

channel ORA_SBT_TAPE_1: reading from backup piece
VB$_1071153822_57811_13

channel ORA_SBT_TAPE_1: piece handle=VB$_1071153822_57811_13
tag=BACKUP_DB12CDB_EXA_021715065526

channel ORA_SBT_TAPE_1: restored backup piece 1

channel ORA_SBT_TAPE_1: restore complete, elapsed time:
00:00:03

channel ORA_SBT_TAPE_1: starting datafile backup set restore

channel ORA_SBT_TAPE_1: specifying datafile(s) to restore from
backup set

channel ORA_SBT_TAPE_1: restoring datafile 00014 to
+DATA/DB12CDB/0C56237BA861F860E0531116C40A9B36/DATAFILE/
users.468.868637093

channel ORA_SBT_TAPE_1: reading from backup piece
VB$_1071153822_57811_14

channel ORA_SBT_TAPE_1: piece handle=VB$_1071153822_57811_14
tag=BACKUP_DB12CDB_EXA_021715065526

channel ORA_SBT_TAPE_1: restored backup piece 1

channel ORA_SBT_TAPE_1: restore complete, elapsed time:
00:00:01

channel ORA_SBT_TAPE_1: starting datafile backup set restore

channel ORA_SBT_TAPE_1: specifying datafile(s) to restore from
backup set

channel ORA_SBT_TAPE_1: restoring datafile 00015 to
+DATA/DB12CDB/0C56237BA861F860E0531116C40A9B36/DATAFILE/
example.469.868637093

channel ORA_SBT_TAPE_1: reading from backup piece
VB$_1071153822_57811_15

channel ORA_SBT_TAPE_1: piece handle=VB$_1071153822_57811_15
tag=BACKUP_DB12CDB_EXA_021715065526

channel ORA_SBT_TAPE_1: restored backup piece 1

channel ORA_SBT_TAPE_1: restore complete, elapsed time:
00:00:03

Finished restore at 2015-02-17 08:11:49

starting full resync of recovery catalog

```
full resync complete

Starting recover at 2015-02-17 08:11:51

using channel ORA_DISK_1

using channel ORA_SBT_TAPE_1

starting media recovery

media recovery complete, elapsed time: 00:00:01

Finished recover at 2015-02-17 08:11:57

RMAN> exit;

Recovery Manager complete.

Now connect as root to CDB and open this database.

SQL> alter pluggable database db12pdb2 open;

Pluggable database altered.
```

Partition Recovery

We will create a partitioned table and then drop a partition.

```
CREATE TABLE "CUST_RAM" ( "CUSTOMER_ID" NUMBER(5),
"CUST_FIRST_NAME" VARCHAR2(10), "CUST_LAST_NAME" VARCHAR2(10),
"CREDIT_LIMIT" NUMBER(5), "DOB" DATE)

PARTITION BY RANGE ("CUSTOMER_ID")

(PARTITION p1 VALUES LESS THAN (1000),

PARTITION p2 VALUES LESS THAN (2000)) ;


insert into cust_ram values
(1100,'RAMESH','RAGHAV',1000,'01-JAN-15');
```

..

```
insert into cust_ram values
(1999,'RAMESH','RAGHAV',1000,'01-JAN-15');


SQL> select * from cust_ram order by customer_id;

100  RAMESH  RAGHAV  1000  01-JAN-15

200  RAMESH  RAGHAV  1000  01-JAN-15

300  RAMESH  RAGHAV  1000  01-JAN-15

400  RAMESH  RAGHAV  1000  01-JAN-15

500  RAMESH  RAGHAV  1000  01-JAN-15

600  RAMESH  RAGHAV  1000  01-JAN-15

700  RAMESH  RAGHAV  1000  01-JAN-15

800  RAMESH  RAGHAV  1000  01-JAN-15

900  RAMESH  RAGHAV  1000  01-JAN-15

999  RAMESH  RAGHAV  1000  01-JAN-15

1100  RAMESH  RAGHAV  1000  01-JAN-15

1200  RAMESH  RAGHAV  1000  01-JAN-15

1300  RAMESH  RAGHAV  1000  01-JAN-15

1400  RAMESH  RAGHAV  1000  01-JAN-15

1500  RAMESH  RAGHAV  1000  01-JAN-15

1600  RAMESH  RAGHAV  1000  01-JAN-15

1700  RAMESH  RAGHAV  1000  01-JAN-15

1800  RAMESH  RAGHAV  1000  01-JAN-15

1900  RAMESH  RAGHAV  1000  01-JAN-15

1999  RAMESH  RAGHAV  1000  01-JAN-15


20 rows selected.


SQL> alter table cust_ram drop partition p2;
```

Table altered.

```
SQL> select * from cust_ram order by customer_id;
100 RAMESH RAGHAV 1000 01-JAN-15

200 RAMESH RAGHAV 1000 01-JAN-15

300 RAMESH RAGHAV 1000 01-JAN-15

400 RAMESH RAGHAV 1000 01-JAN-15

500 RAMESH RAGHAV 1000 01-JAN-15

600 RAMESH RAGHAV 1000 01-JAN-15

700 RAMESH RAGHAV 1000 01-JAN-15

800 RAMESH RAGHAV 1000 01-JAN-15

900 RAMESH RAGHAV 1000 01-JAN-15

999 RAMESH RAGHAV 1000 01-JAN-15


10 rows selected.
```

Now we can restore and recover this partition from the RA backup. The RMAN code snippet below will be used for this task. Please review the output log presented carefully.

```
RMAN> RECOVER TABLE ramesh.cust_ram:p2 OF PLUGGABLE DATABASE
db12pdb2

UNTIL TIME "TO_DATE('28/FEB/2015 12:06:18','DD/MON/YYYY
HH24:MI:SS')"

AUXILIARY DESTINATION '/u01/pochome/part_rec' ;


Recovery Manager: Release 12.1.0.2.0 - Production on Mon Mar 2
15:33:18 2015


Copyright (c) 1982, 2014, Oracle and/or its affiliates. All
rights reserved.


RMAN>
```

connected to target database: DB12CDB (DBID=1943136913)

RMAN>

connected to recovery catalog database

RMAN> 2> 3> 4>

Starting recover at 02-MAR-15

allocated channel: ORA_DISK_1

channel ORA_DISK_1: SID=353 device type=DISK

allocated channel: ORA_SBT_TAPE_1

channel ORA_SBT_TAPE_1: SID=392 device type=SBT_TAPE

channel ORA_SBT_TAPE_1: RA Library (ZDLRA01)
SID=1057A94E36422AD6E0531116C40AA234

Creating automatic instance, with SID='ulxD'

initialization parameters used for automatic instance:

db_name=DB12CDB

db_unique_name=ulxD_pitr_db12pdb2_DB12CDB

compatible=12.1.0.2.0

db_block_size=8192

db_files=200

diagnostic_dest=/u01/app/oracle

_system_trig_enabled=FALSE

sga_target=2560M

processes=200

db_create_file_dest=/u01/pochome/part_rec

log_archive_dest_1='location=/u01/pochome/part_rec'

enable_pluggable_database=true

_clone_one_pdb_recovery=true

#No auxiliary parameter file used

starting up automatic instance DB12CDB

Oracle instance started

Total System Global Area 2684354560 bytes

Fixed Size 2928008 bytes

Variable Size 654312056 bytes

Database Buffers 2013265920 bytes

Redo Buffers 13848576 bytes

Automatic instance created

contents of Memory Script:

```
{
# set requested point in time
set until time "TO_DATE('28/FEB/2015 12:06:18','DD/MON/YYYY
HH24:MI:SS')";
# restore the controlfile
restore clone controlfile;

# mount the controlfile
sql clone 'alter database mount clone database';

# archive current online log
sql 'alter system archive log current';
# resync catalog
resync catalog;
}
executing Memory Script
```

executing command: SET until clause

Starting restore at 02-MAR-15

allocated channel: ORA_AUX_DISK_1

channel ORA_AUX_DISK_1: SID=44 device type=DISK

allocated channel: ORA_AUX_SBT_TAPE_1

channel ORA_AUX_SBT_TAPE_1: SID=58 device type=SBT_TAPE

channel ORA_AUX_SBT_TAPE_1: RA Library (ZDLRA01)
SID=1057AA5214C52C4BE0531116C40A2C37

channel ORA_AUX_SBT_TAPE_1: starting datafile backup set
restore

channel ORA_AUX_SBT_TAPE_1: restoring control file

channel ORA_AUX_SBT_TAPE_1: reading from backup piece
c-1943136913-20150228-00

channel ORA_AUX_SBT_TAPE_1: piece
handle=c-1943136913-20150228-00 tag=TAG20150228T120439

channel ORA_AUX_SBT_TAPE_1: restored backup piece 1

channel ORA_AUX_SBT_TAPE_1: restore complete, elapsed time:
00:00:01

output file name=/u01/pochome/part_rec/DB12CDB/controlfile/
o1_mf_bh9wwzs8_.ctl

Finished restore at 02-MAR-15

sql statement: alter database mount clone database

sql statement: alter system archive log current

starting full resync of recovery catalog
full resync complete

contents of Memory Script:
{

```
# set requested point in time

set until time "TO_DATE('28/FEB/2015 12:06:18','DD/MON/YYYY
HH24:MI:SS')";

# set destinations for recovery set and auxiliary set
datafiles

set newname for clone datafile 1 to new;

set newname for clone datafile 4 to new;

set newname for clone datafile 3 to new;

set newname for clone datafile 12 to new;

set newname for clone datafile 13 to new;

set newname for clone tempfile 1 to new;

set newname for clone tempfile 4 to new;

# switch all tempfiles

switch clone tempfile all;

# restore the tablespaces in the recovery set and the
auxiliary set

restore clone datafile 1, 4, 3, 12, 13;


switch clone datafile all;

}

executing Memory Script


executing command: SET until clause


executing command: SET NEWNAME


executing command: SET NEWNAME


executing command: SET NEWNAME


executing command: SET NEWNAME
```

executing command: SET NEWNAME

executing command: SET NEWNAME

executing command: SET NEWNAME

renamed tempfile 1 to /u01/pochome/part_rec/DB12CDB/datafile/
o1_mf_temp_%u_.tmp in control file

renamed tempfile 4 to /u01/pochome/part_rec/DB12CDB/datafile/
o1_mf_temp_%u_.tmp in control file

Starting restore at 02-MAR-15

using channel ORA_AUX_DISK_1

using channel ORA_AUX_SBT_TAPE_1

channel ORA_AUX_SBT_TAPE_1: starting datafile backup set
restore

channel ORA_AUX_SBT_TAPE_1: specifying datafile(s) to restore
from backup set

channel ORA_AUX_SBT_TAPE_1: restoring datafile 00001 to /u01/
pochome/part_rec/DB12CDB/datafile/o1_mf_system_%u_.dbf

channel ORA_AUX_SBT_TAPE_1: reading from backup piece
VB$_1071153822_79425_1

channel
ORA_AUX_SBT_TAPE_1: piece handle=VB$_1071153822_79425_1
tag=BACKUP_DB12CDB_EXA_022815115804

channel ORA_AUX_SBT_TAPE_1: restored backup piece 1

channel ORA_AUX_SBT_TAPE_1: restore complete, elapsed time:
00:00:07

channel ORA_AUX_SBT_TAPE_1: starting datafile backup set
restore

channel ORA_AUX_SBT_TAPE_1: specifying datafile(s) to restore
from backup set

channel ORA_AUX_SBT_TAPE_1: restoring datafile 00004 to /u01/
pochome/part_rec/DB12CDB/datafile/o1_mf_undotbs1_%u_.dbf

channel ORA_AUX_SBT_TAPE_1: reading from backup piece
VB$_1071153822_79425_4

channel
ORA_AUX_SBT_TAPE_1: piece handle=VB$_1071153822_79425_4
tag=BACKUP_DB12CDB_EXA_022815115804

channel ORA_AUX_SBT_TAPE_1: restored backup piece 1

channel ORA_AUX_SBT_TAPE_1: restore complete, elapsed time:
00:00:07

channel ORA_AUX_SBT_TAPE_1: starting datafile backup set
restore

channel ORA_AUX_SBT_TAPE_1: specifying datafile(s) to restore
from backup set

channel ORA_AUX_SBT_TAPE_1: restoring datafile 00003 to /u01/
pochome/part_rec/DB12CDB/datafile/o1_mf_sysaux_%u_.dbf

channel ORA_AUX_SBT_TAPE_1: reading from backup piece
VB$_1071153822_79425_3

channel
ORA_AUX_SBT_TAPE_1: piece handle=VB$_1071153822_79425_3
tag=BACKUP_DB12CDB_EXA_022815115804

channel ORA_AUX_SBT_TAPE_1: restored backup piece 1

channel ORA_AUX_SBT_TAPE_1: restore complete, elapsed time:
00:00:15

channel ORA_AUX_SBT_TAPE_1: starting datafile backup set
restore

channel ORA_AUX_SBT_TAPE_1: specifying datafile(s) to restore
from backup set

channel ORA_AUX_SBT_TAPE_1: restoring datafile 00012 to /u01/
pochome/part_rec/DB12CDB/datafile/o1_mf_system_%u_.dbf

channel ORA_AUX_SBT_TAPE_1: reading from backup piece
VB$_1071153822_79465_12

channel
ORA_AUX_SBT_TAPE_1: piece handle=VB$_1071153822_79465_12
tag=BACKUP_DB12CDB_EXA_022815115804

channel ORA_AUX_SBT_TAPE_1: restored backup piece 1

channel ORA_AUX_SBT_TAPE_1: restore complete, elapsed time:
00:00:15

channel ORA_AUX_SBT_TAPE_1: starting datafile backup set restore

channel ORA_AUX_SBT_TAPE_1: specifying datafile(s) to restore from backup set

channel ORA_AUX_SBT_TAPE_1: restoring datafile 00013 to /u01/ pochome/part_rec/DB12CDB/datafile/o1_mf_sysaux_%u_.dbf

channel ORA_AUX_SBT_TAPE_1: reading from backup piece VB$_1071153822_79465_13

channel ORA_AUX_SBT_TAPE_1: piece handle=VB$_1071153822_79465_13 tag=BACKUP_DB12CDB_EXA_022815115804

channel ORA_AUX_SBT_TAPE_1: restored backup piece 1

channel ORA_AUX_SBT_TAPE_1: restore complete, elapsed time: 00:00:07

Finished restore at 02-MAR-15

datafile 1 switched to datafile copy

input datafile copy RECID=12 STAMP=873300959 file name=/u01/ pochome/part_rec/DB12CDB/datafile/o1_mf_system_bh9wxf5g_.dbf

datafile 4 switched to datafile copy

input datafile copy RECID=13 STAMP=873300959 file name=/u01/ pochome/part_rec/DB12CDB/datafile/o1_mf_undotbs1_bh9wxm8p_.dbf

datafile 3 switched to datafile copy

input datafile copy RECID=14 STAMP=873300959 file name=/u01/ pochome/part_rec/DB12CDB/datafile/o1_mf_sysaux_bh9wxv8v_.dbf

datafile 12 switched to datafile copy

input datafile copy RECID=15 STAMP=873300959 file name=/u01/ pochome/part_rec/DB12CDB/datafile/o1_mf_system_bh9wybbl_.dbf

datafile 13 switched to datafile copy

input datafile copy RECID=16 STAMP=873300959 file name=/u01/ pochome/part_rec/DB12CDB/datafile/o1_mf_sysaux_bh9wyscz_.dbf

contents of Memory Script:

{

```
# set requested point in time

set until time "TO_DATE('28/FEB/2015 12:06:18','DD/MON/YYYY
HH24:MI:SS')";

# online the datafiles restored or switched

sql clone "alter database datafile 1 online";

sql clone "alter database datafile 4 online";

sql clone "alter database datafile 3 online";

sql clone 'DB12PDB2' "alter database datafile

12 online";

sql clone 'DB12PDB2' "alter database datafile

13 online";

# recover and open database read only

recover clone database tablespace "SYSTEM", "UNDOTBS1",
"SYSAUX", "DB12PDB2":"SYSTEM", "DB12PDB2":"SYSAUX";

sql clone 'alter database open read only';

}

executing Memory Script


executing command: SET until clause


sql statement: alter database datafile 1 online


sql statement: alter database datafile 4 online


sql statement: alter database datafile 3 online


sql statement: alter database datafile 12 online


sql statement: alter database datafile 13 online


Starting recover at 02-MAR-15
```

using channel ORA_AUX_DISK_1

using channel ORA_AUX_SBT_TAPE_1

starting media recovery

archived log for thread 1 with sequence 408 is already on disk as file +RECO/DB12CDB/ARCHIVELOG/2015_02_28/ thread_1_seq_408.2182.872856283

archived log for thread 1 with sequence 409 is already on disk as file +RECO/DB12CDB/ARCHIVELOG/2015_02_28/ thread_1_seq_409.1699.872868751

archived log file name=+RECO/DB12CDB/ARCHIVELOG/2015_02_28/ thread_1_seq_408.2182.872856283 thread=1 sequence=408

archived log file name=+RECO/DB12CDB/ARCHIVELOG/2015_02_28/ thread_1_seq_409.1699.872868751 thread=1 sequence=409

media recovery complete, elapsed time: 00:00:02

Finished recover at 02-MAR-15

sql statement: alter database open read only

contents of Memory Script:

```
{
sql clone 'alter pluggable database DB12PDB2 open read only';
}
```

executing Memory Script

sql statement: alter pluggable database DB12PDB2 open read only

contents of Memory Script:

```
{
sql clone "create spfile from memory";
shutdown clone immediate;
startup clone nomount;
```

```
sql clone "alter system set control_files =

''/u01/pochome/part_rec/DB12CDB/controlfile/o1_mf_bh9wwzs8_.
ctl'' comment=

''RMAN set'' scope=spfile";

shutdown clone immediate;

startup clone nomount;

# mount database

sql clone 'alter database mount clone database';

}

executing Memory Script


sql statement: create spfile from memory


database closed

database dismounted

Oracle instance shut down


connected to auxiliary database (not started)

Oracle instance started


Total System Global Area 2684354560 bytes


Fixed Size 2928008 bytes

Variable Size 671089272 bytes

Database Buffers 1996488704 bytes

Redo Buffers 13848576 bytes


sql statement: alter system set control_files = ''/u01/pochome/
part_rec/DB12CDB/controlfile/o1_mf_bh9wwzs8_.ctl'' comment=
''RMAN set'' scope=spfile


Oracle instance shut down
```

connected to auxiliary database (not started)

Oracle instance started

Total System Global Area 2684354560 bytes

Fixed Size 2928008 bytes

Variable Size 671089272 bytes

Database Buffers 1996488704 bytes

Redo Buffers 13848576 bytes

sql statement: alter database mount clone database

contents of Memory Script:

{

set requested point in time

set until time "TO_DATE('28/FEB/2015 12:06:18','DD/MON/YYYY HH24:MI:SS')";

set destinations for recovery set and auxiliary set datafiles

set newname for datafile 14 to new;

restore the tablespaces in the recovery set and the auxiliary set

restore clone datafile 14;

switch clone datafile all;

}

executing Memory Script

executing command: SET until clause

executing command: SET NEWNAME

Starting restore at 02-MAR-15

allocated channel: ORA_AUX_DISK_1

channel ORA_AUX_DISK_1: SID=44 device type=DISK

allocated channel: ORA_AUX_SBT_TAPE_1

channel ORA_AUX_SBT_TAPE_1: SID=58 device type=SBT_TAPE

channel ORA_AUX_SBT_TAPE_1: RA Library (ZDLRA01)
SID=1057B1DC79813473E0531116C40A7ABD

channel ORA_AUX_SBT_TAPE_1: starting datafile backup set
restore

channel ORA_AUX_SBT_TAPE_1: specifying datafile(s) to restore
from backup set

channel ORA_AUX_SBT_TAPE_1: restoring datafile 00014 to /
u01/pochome/part_rec/ULXD_PITR_DB12PDB2_DB12CDB/datafile/
o1_mf_users_%u_.dbf

channel ORA_AUX_SBT_TAPE_1: reading from backup piece
VB$_1071153822_79465_14

channel
ORA_AUX_SBT_TAPE_1: piece handle=VB$_1071153822_79465_14
tag=BACKUP_DB12CDB_EXA_022815115804

channel ORA_AUX_SBT_TAPE_1: restored backup piece 1

channel ORA_AUX_SBT_TAPE_1: restore complete, elapsed time:
00:00:03

Finished restore at 02-MAR-15

datafile 14 switched to datafile copy

input datafile copy RECID=18 STAMP=873301025 file name=/
u01/pochome/part_rec/ULXD_PITR_DB12PDB2_DB12CDB/datafile/
o1_mf_users_bh9x0zc2_.dbf

contents of Memory Script:

{

set requested point in time

set until time "TO_DATE('28/FEB/2015 12:06:18','DD/MON/YYYY HH24:MI:SS')";

online the datafiles restored or switched

sql clone 'DB12PDB2' "alter database datafile

14 online";

recover and open resetlogs

recover clone database tablespace "DB12PDB2":"USERS", "SYSTEM", "UNDOTBS1", "SYSAUX", "DB12PDB2":"SYSTEM", "DB12PDB2":"SYSAUX" delete archivelog;

alter clone database open resetlogs;

}

executing Memory Script

executing command: SET until clause

sql statement: alter database datafile 14 online

Starting recover at 02-MAR-15

using channel ORA_AUX_DISK_1

using channel ORA_AUX_SBT_TAPE_1

starting media recovery

archived log for thread 1 with sequence 408 is already on disk as file +RECO/DB12CDB/ARCHIVELOG/2015_02_28/ thread_1_seq_408.2182.872856283

archived log for thread 1 with sequence 409 is already on disk as file +RECO/DB12CDB/ARCHIVELOG/2015_02_28/ thread_1_seq_409.1699.872868751

archived log file name=+RECO/DB12CDB/ARCHIVELOG/2015_02_28/ thread_1_seq_408.2182.872856283 thread=1 sequence=408

archived log file name=+RECO/DB12CDB/ARCHIVELOG/2015_02_28/ thread_1_seq_409.1699.872868751 thread=1 sequence=409

media recovery complete, elapsed time: 00:00:03

Finished recover at 02-MAR-15

database opened

contents of Memory Script:
{
sql clone 'alter pluggable database DB12PDB2 open';
}
executing Memory Script

sql statement: alter pluggable database DB12PDB2 open

contents of Memory Script:
{
# create directory for datapump import
sql 'DB12PDB2' "create or replace directory
TSPITR_DIROBJ_DPDIR as ''
/u01/pochome/part_rec'''";
create directory for datapump export
sql clone 'DB12PDB2' "create or replace directory
TSPITR_DIROBJ_DPDIR as ''
/u01/pochome/part_rec'''";
}
executing Memory Script

sql statement: create or replace directory
TSPITR_DIROBJ_DPDIR as ''/u01/pochome/part_rec''

sql statement: create or replace directory
TSPITR_DIROBJ_DPDIR as ''/u01/pochome/part_rec''

Performing export of tables …

EXPDP> Starting "SYS"."TSPITR_EXP_ulxD_atym":

EXPDP> Estimate in progress using BLOCKS method …

EXPDP> Processing object type TABLE_EXPORT/TABLE/TABLE_DATA

EXPDP> Total estimation using BLOCKS method: 8 MB

EXPDP> Processing object type TABLE_EXPORT/TABLE/TABLE

EXPDP> Processing object type TABLE_EXPORT/TABLE/STATISTICS/
TABLE_STATISTICS

EXPDP> Processing object type TABLE_EXPORT/TABLE/STATISTICS/
MARKER

EXPDP> . . exported "RAMESH"."CUST_RAM":"P2" 7.171 KB 10 rows

EXPDP> Master table "SYS"."TSPITR_EXP_ulxD_atym" successfully
loaded/unloaded

EXPDP> ***

EXPDP> Dump file set for SYS.TSPITR_EXP_ulxD_atym is:

EXPDP> /u01/pochome/part_rec/tspitr_ulxD_25948.dmp

EXPDP> Job "SYS"."TSPITR_EXP_ulxD_atym" successfully
completed at Mon Mar 2 15:37:35 2015 elapsed 0 00:00:14

Export completed

contents of Memory Script:

{

shutdown clone before import

shutdown clone abort

}

executing Memory Script

Oracle instance shut down

Performing import of tables …

IMPDP> Master table "SYS"."TSPITR_IMP_ulxD_CcFe" successfully
loaded/unloaded

IMPDP> Starting "SYS"."TSPITR_IMP_ulxD_CcFe":

IMPDP> Processing object type TABLE_EXPORT/TABLE/TABLE

IMPDP> Processing object type TABLE_EXPORT/TABLE/TABLE_DATA

IMPDP> . . imported "RAMESH"."CUST_RAM_P2" 7.171 KB 10 rows

IMPDP> Processing object type TABLE_EXPORT/TABLE/STATISTICS/
MARKER

IMPDP> Job "SYS"."TSPITR_IMP_ulxD_CcFe" successfully
completed at Mon Mar 2 15:37:47 2015 elapsed 0 00:00:06

Import completed

Removing automatic instance

Automatic instance removed

auxiliary instance file /u01/pochome/part_rec/DB12CDB/datafile/
o1_mf_temp_bh9wzdc9_.tmp deleted

auxiliary instance file /u01/pochome/part_rec/DB12CDB/datafile/
o1_mf_temp_bh9wzcky_.tmp deleted

auxiliary instance file /u01/pochome/part_rec/
ULXD_PITR_DB12PDB2_DB12CDB/onlinelog/o1_mf_3_bh9x1bxj_.log
deleted

auxiliary instance file /u01/pochome/part_rec/
ULXD_PITR_DB12PDB2_DB12CDB/onlinelog/o1_mf_2_bh9x1b0x_.log
deleted

auxiliary instance file /u01/pochome/part_rec/
ULXD_PITR_DB12PDB2_DB12CDB/onlinelog/o1_mf_1_bh9x19m5_.log
deleted

auxiliary instance file /u01/pochome/part_rec/
ULXD_PITR_DB12PDB2_DB12CDB/datafile/o1_mf_users_bh9x0zc2_.dbf
deleted

auxiliary instance file /u01/pochome/part_rec/DB12CDB/datafile/
o1_mf_sysaux_bh9wyscz_.dbf deleted

auxiliary instance file /u01/pochome/part_rec/DB12CDB/datafile/
o1_mf_system_bh9wybbl_.dbf deleted

auxiliary instance file /u01/pochome/part_rec/DB12CDB/datafile/
o1_mf_sysaux_bh9wxv8v_.dbf deleted

auxiliary instance file /u01/pochome/part_rec/DB12CDB/datafile/
o1_mf_undotbs1_bh9wxm8p_.dbf deleted

auxiliary instance file /u01/pochome/part_rec/DB12CDB/datafile/
o1_mf_system_bh9wxf5g_.dbf deleted

auxiliary instance file /u01/pochome/part_rec/DB12CDB/
controlfile/o1_mf_bh9wwzs8_.ctl deleted

auxiliary instance file tspitr_ulxD_25948.dmp deleted

Finished recover at 02-MAR-15

RMAN>

Recovery Manager complete.

Now create an empty partition and perform an exchange load.

SQL> alter table cust_ram add partition p2 VALUES LESS THAN
(2000);

SQL> ALTER TABLE cust_ram

EXCHANGE PARTITION p2

WITH TABLE cust_ram_p2;

SQL> select * from cust_ram order by customer_id;

100 RAMESH RAGHAV 1000 01-JAN-15

200 RAMESH RAGHAV 1000 01-JAN-15

300 RAMESH RAGHAV 1000 01-JAN-15

400 RAMESH RAGHAV 1000 01-JAN-15

500 RAMESH RAGHAV 1000 01-JAN-15

600 RAMESH RAGHAV 1000 01-JAN-15

700 RAMESH RAGHAV 1000 01-JAN-15

800 RAMESH RAGHAV 1000 01-JAN-15

900 RAMESH RAGHAV 1000 01-JAN-15

999 RAMESH RAGHAV 1000 01-JAN-15

```
1100 RAMESH RAGHAV 1000 01-JAN-15

1200 RAMESH RAGHAV 1000 01-JAN-15

1300 RAMESH RAGHAV 1000 01-JAN-15

1400 RAMESH RAGHAV 1000 01-JAN-15

1500 RAMESH RAGHAV 1000 01-JAN-15

1600 RAMESH RAGHAV 1000 01-JAN-15

1700 RAMESH RAGHAV 1000 01-JAN-15

1800 RAMESH RAGHAV 1000 01-JAN-15

1900 RAMESH RAGHAV 1000 01-JAN-15

1999 RAMESH RAGHAV 1000 01-JAN-15


20 rows selected.
```

DBPITR

We will now restore/recover a database to the time just before a restore point.

```
RMAN> set dbid 3162507324;
```

executing command: SET DBID

```
RMAN> run {

2> shutdown abort;

3> startup force nomount;

4> set until restore point BEFORE_DELETE;

5> restore controlfile;

6> alter database mount;

7> restore database;

8> recover database;

9> }


channel ORA_SBT_TAPE_1: SID=15 device type=SBT_TAPE
```

channel ORA_SBT_TAPE_1: RA Library (ZDLRA2)
SID=0B28D55EC74CA6CBE053421F4598554C

channel ORA_SBT_TAPE_1: restoring control file

channel ORA_SBT_TAPE_1: reading from backup piece
c-3162507324-20141226-00

channel ORA_SBT_TAPE_1: piece handle=c-3162507324-20141226-00
tag=TAG20141226T171833

channel ORA_SBT_TAPE_1: restored backup piece 1

channel ORA_SBT_TAPE_1: restore complete, elapsed time:
00:00:01

output file name=+REDO/cust01/controlfile/current.293.865501567

channel ORA_SBT_TAPE_1: starting datafile backup set restore

channel ORA_SBT_TAPE_1: specifying datafile(s) to restore from
backup set

channel ORA_SBT_TAPE_1: restoring datafile 00001 to +DATA/
cust01/datafile/system.263.865501577

channel ORA_SBT_TAPE_1: reading from backup piece
VB$_1774727333_82842_1

channel ORA_SBT_TAPE_1: piece handle=VB$_1774727333_82842_1
tag=BACKUP_CUST01_0008_122614051738

channel ORA_SBT_TAPE_1: restored backup piece 1

channel ORA_SBT_TAPE_1: restore complete, elapsed time:
00:00:03

channel ORA_SBT_TAPE_1: starting datafile backup set restore

channel ORA_SBT_TAPE_1: specifying datafile(s) to restore from
backup set

channel ORA_SBT_TAPE_1: restoring datafile 00002 to +DATA/
cust01/datafile/sysaux.336.865501591

channel ORA_SBT_TAPE_1: reading from backup piece
VB$_1774727333_82842_2

channel ORA_SBT_TAPE_1: piece handle=VB$_1774727333_82842_2
tag=BACKUP_CUST01_0008_122614051738

channel ORA_SBT_TAPE_1: restored backup piece 1

channel ORA_SBT_TAPE_1: restore complete, elapsed time: 00:00:03

channel ORA_SBT_TAPE_1: starting datafile backup set restore

channel ORA_SBT_TAPE_1: specifying datafile(s) to restore from backup set

channel ORA_SBT_TAPE_1: restoring datafile 00003 to +DATA/ cust01/datafile/undotbs1.304.865501601

channel ORA_SBT_TAPE_1: reading from backup piece VB$_1774727333_82842_3

channel ORA_SBT_TAPE_1: piece handle=VB$_1774727333_82842_3 tag=BACKUP_CUST01_0008_122614051738

channel ORA_SBT_TAPE_1: restored backup piece 1

channel ORA_SBT_TAPE_1: restore complete, elapsed time: 00:00:07

channel ORA_SBT_TAPE_1: starting datafile backup set restore

channel ORA_SBT_TAPE_1: specifying datafile(s) to restore from backup set

channel ORA_SBT_TAPE_1: restoring datafile 00004 to +DATA/ cust01/datafile/users.337.865501621

channel ORA_SBT_TAPE_1: reading from backup piece VB$_1774727333_82842_4

channel ORA_SBT_TAPE_1: piece handle=VB$_1774727333_82842_4 tag=BACKUP_CUST01_0008_122614051738

channel ORA_SBT_TAPE_1: restored backup piece 1

channel ORA_SBT_TAPE_1: restore complete, elapsed time: 00:00:03

channel ORA_SBT_TAPE_1: starting datafile backup set restore

channel ORA_SBT_TAPE_1: specifying datafile(s) to restore from backup set

channel ORA_SBT_TAPE_1: restoring datafile 00005 to +DATA/ cust01/datafile/soe.dbf

channel ORA_SBT_TAPE_1: reading from backup piece VB$_1774727333_82842_5

channel ORA_SBT_TAPE_1: piece handle=VB$_1774727333_82842_5 tag=BACKUP_CUST01_0008_122614051738 channel ORA_SBT_TAPE_1: restored backup piece 1

channel ORA_SBT_TAPE_1: restore complete, elapsed time: 00:00:07

Finished restore at 2014-12-26 17:37:10

starting media recovery

channel ORA_SBT_TAPE_1: starting archived log restore to default destination

channel ORA_SBT_TAPE_1: restoring archived log

archived log thread=1 sequence=8

channel ORA_SBT_TAPE_1: reading from backup piece I_ARC$+DELTA/ZDLRA2/ARCHIVELOG/2014_12_25/ thread_1_seq_8.521.867260539

channel ORA_SBT_TAPE_1: piece handle=I_ARC$+DELTA/ ZDLRA2/ARCHIVELOG/2014_12_25/thread_1_seq_8.521.867260539 tag=TAG20141226T173603

channel ORA_SBT_TAPE_1: restored backup piece 1

channel ORA_SBT_TAPE_1: restore complete, elapsed time: 00:00:07

archived log file name=+RECO/cust01/archivelog/2014_12_26/ thread_1_seq_8.2184.867346637 thread=1 sequence=8

channel default: deleting archived log(s)

archived log file name=+RECO/cust01/archivelog/2014_12_26/ thread_1_seq_8.2184.867346637 RECID=180 STAMP=867346641

media recovery complete, elapsed time: 00:00:00

Finished recover at 2014-12-26 17:37:23

RMAN> alter database open resetlogs;

database opened

new incarnation of database registered in recovery catalog

starting full resync of recovery catalog

full resync complete

CHANGE TRACKING is reinitializing the change tracking file.

Starting background process CTWR

Fri Dec 26 17:37:38 2014

CTWR started with pid=37, OS id=46310

Block change tracking service is active.

TSPITR

We will now restore/recover a tablespace to the time just before a restore point.

Recovery Manager: Release 11.2.0.4.0 - Production on Sat Dec 27 09:43:33 2014

Copyright (c) 1982, 2011, Oracle and/or its affiliates. All rights reserved.

RMAN>

connected to target database: CUST01 (DBID=3162507324)

RMAN>

connected to recovery catalog database

RMAN>

echo set on

RMAN> run {

2> sql 'alter system archive log current';

3> recover tablespace 'SOE' until restore point 'BEFORE_TSPITR' auxiliary destination = '/u01/app/oracle/admin/cust01/aux'

4> ;

5> backup tablespace 'SOE';

6> sql 'alter tablespace "SOE" online';

7> }

sql statement: alter system archive log current

Starting recover at 2014-12-27 09:43:35

allocated channel: ORA_SBT_TAPE_1

channel ORA_SBT_TAPE_1: SID=35 device type=SBT_TAPE

channel ORA_SBT_TAPE_1: RA Library (ZDLRA2)
SID=0B3657B84FEA9EC2E053421F45985ECF

allocated channel: ORA_DISK_1

channel ORA_DISK_1: SID=197 device type=DISK

Creating automatic instance, with SID='Ccch'

initialization parameters used for automatic instance:

db_name=CUST01

db_unique_name=Ccch_tspitr_CUST01

compatible=11.2.0.4.0

db_block_size=8192

db_files=1024

sga_target=1G

processes=80

db_create_file_dest=/u01/app/oracle/admin/cust01/aux

log_archive_dest_1='location=/u01/app/oracle/admin/cust01/aux'

#No auxiliary parameter file used

starting up automatic instance CUST01

Oracle instance started

Total System Global Area 1068937216 bytes

Fixed Size 2260088 bytes

Variable Size 285213576 bytes

Database Buffers 759169024 bytes

Redo Buffers 22294528 bytes

Automatic instance created

Running TRANSPORT_SET_CHECK on recovery set tablespaces

TRANSPORT_SET_CHECK completed successfully

contents of Memory Script:

{

set requested point in time

set until scn 3245820;

restore the controlfile

restore clone controlfile;

mount the controlfile

sql clone 'alter database mount clone database';

archive current online log

sql 'alter system archive log current';

avoid unnecessary autobackups for structural changes
during TSPITR

sql 'begin dbms_backup_restore.AutoBackupFlag(FALSE); end;';

resync catalog

resync catalog;

}

executing Memory Script

executing command: SET until clause

Starting restore at 2014-12-27 09:44:18

allocated channel: ORA_AUX_SBT_TAPE_1

channel ORA_AUX_SBT_TAPE_1: SID=91 device type=SBT_TAPE

channel ORA_AUX_SBT_TAPE_1: RA Library (ZDLRA2)
SID=0B365A3EF84CA94CE053421F45982727

allocated channel: ORA_AUX_DISK_1

channel ORA_AUX_DISK_1: SID=94 device type=DISK

channel ORA_AUX_SBT_TAPE_1: starting datafile backup set
restore

channel ORA_AUX_SBT_TAPE_1: restoring control file

channel ORA_AUX_SBT_TAPE_1: reading from backup piece
c-3162507324-20141227-00

channel ORA_AUX_SBT_TAPE_1: piece
handle=c-3162507324-20141227-00 tag=TAG20141227T090528

channel ORA_AUX_SBT_TAPE_1: restored backup piece 1

channel ORA_AUX_SBT_TAPE_1: restore complete, elapsed time:
00:00:01

output file name=/u01/app/oracle/admin/cust01/aux/CUST01/
controlfile/o1_mf_b9xrh4hs_.ctl

Finished restore at 2014-12-27 09:44:21

sql statement: alter database mount clone database

sql statement: alter system archive log current

sql statement: begin dbms_backup_restore.
AutoBackupFlag(FALSE); end;

starting full resync of recovery catalog

full resync complete

contents of Memory Script:

{

set requested point in time

```
set until scn 3245820;

# set destinations for recovery set and auxiliary set
datafiles

set newname for clone datafile 1 to new;

set newname for clone datafile 3 to new;

set newname for clone datafile 2 to new;

set newname for clone tempfile 1 to new;

set newname for datafile 5 to

"+DATA/cust01/datafile/soe.dbf";

# switch all tempfiles

switch clone tempfile all;

# restore the tablespaces in the recovery set and the
auxiliary set

restore clone datafile 1, 3, 2, 5;

switch clone datafile all;

}

executing Memory Script


executing command: SET until clause


executing command: SET NEWNAME


executing command: SET NEWNAME


executing command: SET NEWNAME


executing command: SET NEWNAME


executing command: SET NEWNAME


renamed tempfile 1 to /u01/app/oracle/admin/cust01/aux/CUST01/
datafile/o1_mf_temp_%u_.tmp in control file
```

Starting restore at 2014-12-27 09:44:29

using channel ORA_AUX_SBT_TAPE_1

using channel ORA_AUX_DISK_1

channel ORA_AUX_SBT_TAPE_1: starting datafile backup set restore

channel ORA_AUX_SBT_TAPE_1: specifying datafile(s) to restore from backup set

channel ORA_AUX_SBT_TAPE_1: restoring datafile 00001 to /u01/app/oracle/admin/cust01/aux/CUST01/datafile/ o1_mf_system_%u_.dbf

channel ORA_AUX_SBT_TAPE_1: reading from backup piece VB$_1774727333_86332_1

channel ORA_AUX_SBT_TAPE_1: piece handle=VB$_1774727333_86332_1 tag=BACKUP_CUST01_0008_122714090410

channel ORA_AUX_SBT_TAPE_1: restored backup piece 1

channel ORA_AUX_SBT_TAPE_1: restore complete, elapsed time: 00:00:15

channel ORA_AUX_SBT_TAPE_1: starting datafile backup set restore

channel ORA_AUX_SBT_TAPE_1: specifying datafile(s) to restore from backup set

channel ORA_AUX_SBT_TAPE_1: restoring datafile 00003 to /u01/app/oracle/admin/cust01/aux/CUST01/datafile/ o1_mf_undotbs1_%u_.dbf

channel ORA_AUX_SBT_TAPE_1: reading from backup piece VB$_1774727333_86332_3

channel ORA_AUX_SBT_TAPE_1: piece handle=VB$_1774727333_86332_3 tag=BACKUP_CUST01_0008_122714090410

channel ORA_AUX_SBT_TAPE_1: restored backup piece 1

channel ORA_AUX_SBT_TAPE_1: restore complete, elapsed time: 00:00:15

channel ORA_AUX_SBT_TAPE_1: starting datafile backup set restore

channel ORA_AUX_SBT_TAPE_1: specifying datafile(s) to restore
from backup set

channel ORA_AUX_SBT_TAPE_1: restoring datafile 00002
to /u01/app/oracle/admin/cust01/aux/CUST01/datafile/
o1_mf_sysaux_%u_.dbf

channel ORA_AUX_SBT_TAPE_1: reading from backup piece
VB$_1774727333_86332_2

channel
ORA_AUX_SBT_TAPE_1: piece handle=VB$_1774727333_86332_2
tag=BACKUP_CUST01_0008_122714090410

channel ORA_AUX_SBT_TAPE_1: restored backup piece 1

channel ORA_AUX_SBT_TAPE_1: restore complete, elapsed time:
00:00:15

channel ORA_AUX_SBT_TAPE_1: starting datafile backup set
restore

channel ORA_AUX_SBT_TAPE_1: specifying datafile(s) to restore
from backup set

channel ORA_AUX_SBT_TAPE_1: restoring datafile 00005 to +DATA/
cust01/datafile/soe.dbf

channel ORA_AUX_SBT_TAPE_1: reading from backup piece
VB$_1774727333_86332_5

channel
ORA_AUX_SBT_TAPE_1: piece handle=VB$_1774727333_86332_5
tag=BACKUP_CUST01_0008_122714090410

channel ORA_AUX_SBT_TAPE_1: restored backup piece 1

channel ORA_AUX_SBT_TAPE_1: restore complete, elapsed time:
00:00:07

Finished restore at 2014-12-27 09:45:25

datafile 1 switched to datafile copy

input datafile copy RECID=4 STAMP=867404726 file name=/
u01/app/oracle/admin/cust01/aux/CUST01/datafile/
o1_mf_system_b9xrhm1r_.dbf

datafile 3 switched to datafile copy

input datafile copy RECID=5 STAMP=867404726 file name=/
u01/app/oracle/admin/cust01/aux/CUST01/datafile/
o1_mf_undotbs1_b9xrj23t_.dbf

datafile 2 switched to datafile copy

input datafile copy RECID=6 STAMP=867404726 file name=/
u01/app/oracle/admin/cust01/aux/CUST01/datafile/
o1_mf_sysaux_b9xrjk54_.dbf

contents of Memory Script:

{

set requested point in time

set until scn 3245820;

online the datafiles restored or switched

sql clone "alter database datafile 1 online";

sql clone "alter database datafile 3 online";

sql clone "alter database datafile 2 online";

sql clone "alter database datafile 5 online";

recover and open resetlogs

recover clone database tablespace "SOE", "SYSTEM", "UNDOTBS1",
"SYSAUX" delete archivelog;

alter clone database open resetlogs;

}

executing Memory Script

executing command: SET until clause

sql statement: alter database datafile 1 online

sql statement: alter database datafile 3 online

sql statement: alter database datafile 2 online

sql statement: alter database datafile 5 online

Starting recover at 2014-12-27 09:45:26

using channel ORA_AUX_SBT_TAPE_1

using channel ORA_AUX_DISK_1

starting media recovery

archived log for thread 1 with sequence 3 is already
on disk as file +RECO/cust01/archivelog/2014_12_27/
thread_1_seq_3.2252.867403715

archived log file name=+RECO/cust01/archivelog/2014_12_27/
thread_1_seq_3.2252.867403715 thread=1 sequence=3

media recovery complete, elapsed time: 00:00:00

Finished recover at 2014-12-27 09:45:28

database opened

contents of Memory Script:
{
# make read only the tablespace that will be exported
sql clone 'alter tablespace "SOE" read only';
create directory for datapump import
sql "create or replace directory TSPITR_DIROBJ_DPDIR as ''
/u01/app/oracle/admin/cust01/aux''";
create directory for datapump export
sql clone "create or replace directory
TSPITR_DIROBJ_DPDIR as ''
/u01/app/oracle/admin/cust01/aux''";
}
executing Memory Script

sql statement: alter tablespace "SOE" read only

sql statement: create or replace directory
TSPITR_DIROBJ_DPDIR as ''/u01/app/oracle/admin/cust01/aux''

sql statement: create or replace directory
TSPITR_DIROBJ_DPDIR as ''/u01/app/oracle/admin/cust01/aux''

Performing export of metadata ...

EXPDP> Starting "SYS"."TSPITR_EXP_Ccch":

EXPDP> Processing object type TRANSPORTABLE_EXPORT/PLUGTS_BLK

EXPDP> Processing object type TRANSPORTABLE_EXPORT/TABLE

EXPDP> Processing object type TRANSPORTABLE_EXPORT/
CONSTRAINT/CONSTRAINT

EXPDP> Processing object type TRANSPORTABLE_EXPORT/
TABLE_STATISTICS

EXPDP> Processing object type TRANSPORTABLE_EXPORT/
USER_PREF_STATISTICS

EXPDP> Processing object type TRANSPORTABLE_EXPORT/
POST_INSTANCE/PLUGTS_BLK

EXPDP> Master table "SYS"."TSPITR_EXP_Ccch" successfully
loaded/unloaded

EXPDP> **

EXPDP> Dump file set for SYS.TSPITR_EXP_Ccch is:

EXPDP> /u01/app/oracle/admin/cust01/aux/tspitr_Ccch_86224.dmp

EXPDP> **

EXPDP> Datafiles required for transportable tablespace SOE:

EXPDP> +DATA/cust01/datafile/soe.dbf

EXPDP> Job "SYS"."TSPITR_EXP_Ccch" successfully completed at
Sat Dec 27 09:46:27 2014 elapsed 0 00:00:16

Export completed

contents of Memory Script:

```
{

# shutdown clone before import

shutdown clone immediate

# drop target tablespaces before importing them back

sql 'drop tablespace "SOE" including contents keep datafiles
cascade constraints';

}
```

executing Memory Script

database closed

database dismounted

Oracle instance shut down

sql statement: drop tablespace "SOE" including contents keep
datafiles cascade constraints

Performing import of metadata …

IMPDP> Master table "SYS"."TSPITR_IMP_Ccch" successfully
loaded/unloaded

IMPDP> Starting "SYS"."TSPITR_IMP_Ccch":

IMPDP> Processing object type TRANSPORTABLE_EXPORT/PLUGTS_BLK

IMPDP> Processing object type TRANSPORTABLE_EXPORT/TABLE

IMPDP> Processing object type TRANSPORTABLE_EXPORT/
CONSTRAINT/CONSTRAINT

IMPDP> Processing object type TRANSPORTABLE_EXPORT/
TABLE_STATISTICS

IMPDP> Processing object type TRANSPORTABLE_EXPORT/
USER_PREF_STATISTICS

IMPDP> Processing object type TRANSPORTABLE_EXPORT/
POST_INSTANCE/PLUGTS_BLK

IMPDP> Job "SYS"."TSPITR_IMP_Ccch" successfully completed at
Sat Dec 27 09:47:00 2014 elapsed 0 00:00:16

Import completed

contents of Memory Script:

{

make read write and offline the imported tablespaces

sql 'alter tablespace "SOE" read write';

sql 'alter tablespace "SOE" offline';

enable autobackups after TSPITR is finished

sql 'begin dbms_backup_restore.AutoBackupFlag(TRUE); end;';

resync catalog

resync catalog;

}

executing Memory Script

sql statement: alter tablespace "SOE" read write

sql statement: alter tablespace "SOE" offline

sql statement: begin dbms_backup_restore.
AutoBackupFlag(TRUE); end;

starting full resync of recovery catalog

full resync complete

Removing automatic instance

Automatic instance removed

auxiliary instance file /u01/app/oracle/admin/cust01/aux/
CUST01/datafile/o1_mf_temp_b9xrlccp_.tmp deleted

auxiliary instance file /u01/app/oracle/admin/cust01/aux/
CUST01/onlinelog/o1_mf_3_b9xrkyro_.log deleted

auxiliary instance file /u01/app/oracle/admin/cust01/aux/
CUST01/onlinelog/o1_mf_2_b9xrkmpk_.log deleted

auxiliary instance file /u01/app/oracle/admin/cust01/aux/
CUST01/onlinelog/o1_mf_1_b9xrk8yo_.log deleted

auxiliary instance file /u01/app/oracle/admin/cust01/aux/ CUST01/datafile/o1_mf_sysaux_b9xrjk54_.dbf deleted

auxiliary instance file /u01/app/oracle/admin/cust01/aux/ CUST01/datafile/o1_mf_undotbs1_b9xrj23t_.dbf deleted

auxiliary instance file /u01/app/oracle/admin/cust01/aux/ CUST01/datafile/o1_mf_system_b9xrhm1r_.dbf deleted

auxiliary instance file /u01/app/oracle/admin/cust01/aux/ CUST01/controlfile/o1_mf_b9xrh4hs_.ctl deleted

Finished recover at 2014-12-27 09:47:06

Starting backup at 2014-12-27 09:47:07

released channel: ORA_DISK_1

using channel ORA_SBT_TAPE_1

channel ORA_SBT_TAPE_1: starting full datafile backup set

channel ORA_SBT_TAPE_1: specifying datafile(s) in backup set

input datafile file number=00005 name=+DATA/cust01/datafile/ soe.dbf

channel ORA_SBT_TAPE_1: starting piece 1 at 2014-12-27 09:47:08

channel ORA_SBT_TAPE_1: finished piece 1 at 2014-12-27 09:47:15

piece handle=8rpr730s_1_1 tag=TAG20141227T094707 comment=API Version 2.0,MMS Version 3.14.10.26

channel ORA_SBT_TAPE_1: backup set complete, elapsed time: 00:00:07

Finished backup at 2014-12-27 09:47:15

Starting Control File and SPFILE Autobackup at 2014-12-27 09:47:15

piece handle=c-3162507324-20141227-01 comment=API Version 2.0,MMS Version 3.14.10.26

Finished Control File and SPFILE Autobackup at 2014-12-27 09:47:17

starting full resync of recovery catalog

full resync complete

sql statement: alter tablespace "SOE" online

starting full resync of recovery catalog

full resync complete

RMAN> exit;

Recovery Manager complete.

Restore from Replica

Backup pieces will be retrieved from the downstream RA if they are not available upstream.

Please note the 4th piece handle for restore of users tablespace datafile below.

channel ORA_SBT_TAPE_1: starting datafile backup set restore

channel ORA_SBT_TAPE_1: specifying datafile(s) to restore from backup set

channel ORA_SBT_TAPE_1: restoring datafile 00001 to +DATA/cust01/datafile/system.263.865501577

channel ORA_SBT_TAPE_1: reading from backup piece VB$_1774727333_103858_1

channel ORA_SBT_TAPE_1: piece handle=VB$_1774727333_103858_1 tag=BACKUP_CUST01_0008_123014085556

channel ORA_SBT_TAPE_1: restored backup piece 1

channel ORA_SBT_TAPE_1: restore complete, elapsed time: 00:00:03

channel ORA_SBT_TAPE_1: starting datafile backup set restore

channel ORA_SBT_TAPE_1: specifying datafile(s) to restore from backup set

channel ORA_SBT_TAPE_1: restoring datafile 00002 to +DATA/cust01/datafile/sysaux.336.865501591

channel ORA_SBT_TAPE_1: reading from backup piece VB$_1774727333_103858_2

channel ORA_SBT_TAPE_1: piece handle=VB$_1774727333_103858_2
tag=BACKUP_CUST01_0008_123014085556

channel ORA_SBT_TAPE_1: restored backup piece 1

channel ORA_SBT_TAPE_1: restore complete, elapsed time:
00:00:07

channel ORA_SBT_TAPE_1: starting datafile backup set restore

channel ORA_SBT_TAPE_1: specifying datafile(s) to restore from
backup set

channel ORA_SBT_TAPE_1: restoring datafile 00003 to +DATA/
cust01/datafile/undotbs1.304.865501601

channel ORA_SBT_TAPE_1: reading from backup piece
VB$_1774727333_103858_3

channel ORA_SBT_TAPE_1: piece handle=VB$_1774727333_103858_3
tag=BACKUP_CUST01_0008_123014085556

channel ORA_SBT_TAPE_1: restored backup piece 1

channel ORA_SBT_TAPE_1: restore complete, elapsed time:
00:00:03

channel ORA_SBT_TAPE_1: starting datafile backup set restore

channel ORA_SBT_TAPE_1: specifying datafile(s) to restore from
backup set

channel ORA_SBT_TAPE_1: restoring datafile 00004 to +DATA/
cust01/datafile/users.337.867406917

channel ORA_SBT_TAPE_1: reading from backup piece
VB$_2090147041_57694_4

channel ORA_SBT_TAPE_1: piece handle=VB$_2090147041_57694_4
tag=BACKUP_CUST01_0008_123014085556

channel ORA_SBT_TAPE_1: restored backup piece 1

channel ORA_SBT_TAPE_1: restore complete, elapsed time:
00:00:07

channel ORA_SBT_TAPE_1: starting datafile backup set restore

channel ORA_SBT_TAPE_1: specifying datafile(s) to restore from
backup set

channel ORA_SBT_TAPE_1: restoring datafile 00005 to +DATA/
cust01/datafile/soe.dbf

channel ORA_SBT_TAPE_1: reading from backup piece
VB$_1774727333_103858_5

channel ORA_SBT_TAPE_1: piece handle=VB$_1774727333_103858_5
tag=BACKUP_CUST01_0008_123014085556

channel ORA_SBT_TAPE_1: restored backup piece 1

channel ORA_SBT_TAPE_1: restore complete, elapsed time:
00:00:15

Finished restore at 2014-12-30 10:21:16

Recovering RA catalog

A background process on the system backs up the necessary EM agent, OSB catalog, and Recovery Appliance catalog information (e.g. backup metadata, protected database/VPC users, protection policies, etc.) every 2 hours alternating between nodes. In the event of a complete system failure, this backup is used to recover the Recovery Appliance catalog, along with all users and policies as of the time the backup was taken.

The export process is controlled by ra_export.pl script, which is run by root user.

/opt/oracle.RecoveryAppliance/bin/ra_export.pl

These dumps will be named /dbfs_obdbfs/OSB/ra_export/ra_backup.YYYYDD. HMM.*.tar.gz.

(like ra_backup.201528.830.3794.tar.gz)

The export bundle files are automatically cleaned up. 48 of these are retained (4 day duration) in a rolling window manner. Place the desired export bundle file in /opt/oracle.RecoveryAppliance/import prior to running ra_install script and all needed data will be automatically imported.

Tip: Copy the most recent export bundle to an external storage periodically (atleast once a day).

12

Maintenance and Performance

In this chapter we will cover certain miscellaneous topics of general interest pertaining to the Recovery Appliance.

Powering down RA

Connect to metadata database as user RASYS using sqlplus.

```
SQL> SELECT state FROM ra_server;

STATE

------------

ON


SQL> exec dbms_ra.shutdown;
```

If OSB is configured, shut down the cluster resource as root user.

```
# $GRID_HOME/bin/crsctl status res osbadmin

NAME=osbadmin

TYPE=cluster_resource

TARGET=ONLINE

STATE=ONLINE on slcm03adm03


# $GRID_HOME/bin/crsctl stop res osbadmin
```

As oracle user check status of DataBaseFileSystem(DBFS) mounts.

```
$ $GRID_HOME/bin/crsctl status res ob_dbfs rep_dbfs
NAME=ob_dbfs
TYPE=local_resource
TARGET=ONLINE , ONLINE
STATE=ONLINE on slcm03adm03, ONLINE on slcm03adm04

NAME=rep_dbfs
TYPE=local_resource
TARGET=ONLINE , ONLINE
STATE=ONLINE on slcm03adm03, ONLINE on slcm03adm04

$ $GRID_HOME/bin/crsctl stop res ob_dbfs rep_dbfs
```

Check status of catalog database.

```
$ srvctl status database -d zdlra2
Instance zdlra21 is running on node slcm03adm03
Instance zdlra22 is running on node slcm03adm04

$ srvctl stop database -d zdlra2
```

As root user stop cluster on all compute nodes.

```
# $GRID_HOME/bin/crsctl stop cluster -all
```

On each compute node stop CRS.

```
# $GRID_HOME/bin/crsctl stop crs
```

Using dcli shutdown remote compute node.

```
# dcli -l root -g .. shutdown -h- y now
```

Shutdown storage cells.

```
# dcli -l root -g cell_group shutdown -h -y now
```

Finally, shutdown local compute node.

```
# shutdown -h -y now
```

For powering up RA, follow this sequence:

Start the switches and wait a few minutes for them to initialize.

Start the storage cells.

(Wait for about 10 minutes for start of all services)

Start the compute nodes and Oracle Clusterware will start all resources automatically.

Ingest over IB for Exadata DataBase Machine

Ensure that the RA **AND** Exadata racks in the InfiniBand fabric are in the same subnet and have unique IP addresses.

Edit the /etc/hosts file on all servers in the InfiniBand fabric to list all IP addresses and hostnames.

Cable the Recovery Appliance and Exadata Database Machine racks together.

Add a new network to Oracle Clusterware and create a VIP for each compute server in the Recovery Appliance rack pertaining to IB.

```
[oracle@slcm03adm01 ~]$ $GRID_HOME/bin/oifcfg iflist -p -n|grep PRIVATE

ib0 192.168.10.0 PRIVATE 255.255.255.0

ib1 192.168.10.0 PRIVATE 255.255.255.0
```

As root user add this network and VIPs.

```
# srvctl add network -k 3 -S 192.168.10.0/255.255.255.0/ib0\|ib1
```

```
# srvctl add vip -n slcm03adm03 -A slcm03adm03-priv.
us.oracle.com/255.255.255.0/ib0\|ib1 -k 3
```

```
# srvctl add vip -n slcm03adm04 -A slcm03adm04-priv.
us.oracle.com/255.255.255.0/ib0\|ib1 -k 3
```

```
# srvctl start vip -i slcm03adm03-priv.us.oracle.com
```

```
# srvctl start vip -i slcm03adm04-priv.us.oracle.com
```

As oracle user verify VIPs are running.

```
$ srvctl status slcm03adm03-priv.us.oracle.com
```

```
VIP 192.168.10.6 is enabled
```

```
VIP 192.168.10.6 is running on node:slcm03adm03.us.oracle.com
```

```
$ srvctl status slcm03adm04-priv.us.oracle.com
```

```
VIP 192.168.10.7 is enabled
```

```
VIP 192.168.10.7 is running on node:slcm03adm04.us.oracle.com
```

10GbE is the default network but now we have to make InfiniBand as the preferred network.

Connect to metadata database as user RASYS using sqlplus.

```
SQL> desc rasys.rai_host
```

```
Name Null? Type
```

```
-------------------------------- -------- -----------------------
```

```
NODE_NAME NOT NULL VARCHAR2(256)
```

```
ADMIN_IP_ADDRESS NOT NULL VARCHAR2(4000)
```

```
BACKUP_IP_ADDRESS NOT NULL VARCHAR2(4000)
```

```
REPLICATION_IP_ADDRESS VARCHAR2(4000)
```

```
SQL> UPDATE rai_host
SET backup_ip_address='192.168.10.6,'||backup_ip_address
WHERE node_name='slcm03adm03.us.oracle.com';
```

```
SQL> UPDATE rai_host

SET backup_ip_address='192.168.10.7,'||backup_ip_address

WHERE node_name='slcm03adm04.us.oracle.com';


SQL> ALTER SYSTEM SET dispatchers=

'(DESCRIPTION=(ADDRESS=(PROTOCOL=TCP)

(HOST= slcm03adm03-priv.us.oracle.com))(SDU=65536))

(SERVICE=ZDLRA2XDB)(DISPATCHERS=10)' SCOPE=BOTH SID='zdlra21';


SQL> ALTER SYSTEM SET dispatchers=

'(DESCRIPTION=(ADDRESS=(PROTOCOL=TCP)

(HOST= slcm03adm04-priv.us.oracle.com))(SDU=65536))

(SERVICE=ZDLRA2XDB)(DISPATCHERS=10)' SCOPE=BOTH SID='zdlra22';
```

Migrating backups to RA

We can also migrate pre-existing backups to the Recovery Appliance.

First, the backup metadata has to be moved.

Connect to SQL*Plus as the source recovery catalog owner that stores metadata for the protected database.

```
SQL> SELECT COUNT(*) FROM rc_backup_piece_details WHERE
db_name='FINPRD';
```

Using RMAN verify the integrity of backups by restoring them or by using the RESTORE .. VALIDATE command.

The version of source RMAN recovery catalog schema must be equal to the current version of the RA recovery catalog schema (12.1.0.2). Hence upgrade the source recovery catalog schema to 12.1.0.2 if needed.

Connect to SQL*Plus as the recovery catalog owner and run the dbmsrmansys. sql script.

($ORACLE_HOME/rdbms/admin/dbmsrmansys.sql)

Import the source catalog into the RA recovery catalog.

Connect to RMAN as CATALOG using the rasys user. Now connect to source catalog also.

```
RMAN> IMPORT CATALOG src_cat11/reco4prd@prdcat11 DB_NAME
'FINPRD' NO UNREGISTER;
```

Verify that all the backup pieces are included in the Recovery Appliance catalog by querying the RC_BACKUP_PIECE_DETAILS view.

Next, we migrate the backups to RA.

Connect to metadata database as user RASYS using sqlplus and create the polling policy.

```
BEGIN

DBMS_RA.CREATE_POLLING_POLICY (

polling_policy_name => 'RA_POLL',

polling_location => '/ra_polling',

polling_frequency => INTERVAL '30' MINUTE,

delete_input => FALSE);

END;
```

Now run the DBMS_RA.UPDATE_PROTECTION_POLICY procedure to assign this polling policy.

It is time now to mount the NFS storage holding the backups at the ra_polling directory

Also, you can use the dbms_ra.migrate_tape_backup procedure to make pre-migration tape backups available to the Recovery Appliance through the specified SBT library. You must first import metadata about the tape backups into the Recovery Appliance catalog using the RMAN IMPORT CATALOG command.

```
PROCEDURE MIGRATE_TAPE_BACKUP
```

```
Argument Name Type In/Out Default?

------------------------ ----------------------- ------ --------

DB_UNIQUE_NAME VARCHAR2 IN

SBT_LIB_NAME VARCHAR2 IN
```

Updating validation checks

Connect to metadata database as user RASYS using sqlplus.

You may then execute dbms_ra.config procedure to update values for parameters.

```
PROCEDURE CONFIG

Argument Name Type In/Out Default?

------------------------ ----------------------- ------ --------

P_NAME VARCHAR2 IN

P_VALUE VARCHAR2 IN
```

The key checks are:

- check_file_days is the frequency of background metadata consistency checks (defaults to 14 days)

- crosscheck_db_days is the frequency of background updates of recovery catalog to sync up with tape libraries or downstream Recovery Appliances (defaults to 1 day)

- optimize_chunks_days is the frequency of background reordering of blocks in delta store to reduce disk reads for restore (defaults to 7 days)

- validate_db_days is the frequency of background validation of backup pieces (defaults to 14 days)

Performance PoV

For a large Financial customer, Oracle executed the proof of concept (or value) exercise to net out performance numbers for the Recovery Appliance. This customer has a database estate of about 16,000 (yes, indeed) Oracle databases spanning versions 10g to 12c !

In their environment the RMAN backups to local SAN/NAS "dump" storage have a retention of 2 weeks.

The disk backups are then swept weekly by NetBackup to Data Domain for a 30-day retention period.

The backups are also copied to physical tape for databases where retention is needed beyond 30 days.

The customer has these major pain points with their current strategy.

- Very large & expensive "dump" storage deployed for 16,000 databases

- Inability to coordinate NetBackup sweep schedule with RMAN backups, resulting in incomplete backups and restore failures

- Non-Oracle integrated tape backup strategy resulting in RTO exceeding 48 hours

The pervasive risk of recovery failure and/or data loss directly translated into statutory non-compliance, heavy dollar penalties, and bad press.

For the PoV exercise, the configuration details are as follows:

200 protected databases (single instance)

−160 databases on Oracle 11.2.0.4 with redo transport to the Recovery Appliance

−20 databases on Oracle 11.1.0.7

−20 databases on Oracle 10.2.0.5

−Average Database Size = 450 GB with 30+ data files

These were hosted on

−1x Exadata full rack X3-2 with HP drives (64 databases)

−3x Exadata half rack X2-2 with HP drives (96 databases)

−2x X4800 M2 + ZFS Storage (40 databases)

−10 Gb/s network interfaces for backups

−Recovery Appliance X5 with 2 compute nodes and 18 storage cells configured with LACP providing a total of 40 Gb/sec ingest network bandwidth

–Two StorageTek SL150 tape libraries with two LTO6 drives in each, connected to the Recovery Appliance via Fibre Channel

–Oracle Enterprise Manager 12c (12.1.0.4) with RA plugin

The following test cases were evaluated:

1 Execute level 0 backup on 200 protected databases

This was completed in 6 hours and 17 minutes, 4X faster than customer stipulated requirement. Backup rate was 14.7 TB/hour (4.2 GB/sec).

2 Copy 200 database backups to tape in 7 days

After the level 0 backups, a workload generation script was executed to effect ~12% random block changes in each database. Upon completion, level 1 backups were taken on all databases.

A total of 6960 tape backup tasks was executed with a throughput of 125MB/sec/ tape drive.

The backup to tape was completed in 2 days and 3 hours, 3X faster than customer stipulated requirement.

3 Real-time redo transport with RPO < 5 seconds

160 databases were being updated with 12% change rate.

The RPO (unprotected data window) was consistently < 1 sec for all these databases.

4 Complete level 1 backups within 8 hours

A 12% load process ran against all the databases to update data and level 1 incremental backups were then taken.

All level 1 backups completed and were ingested by the Recovery Appliance in 2.5 hours, 3X faster than the customer stipulated requirement. The effective backup rate was 32 TB/hour.

In all the above cases, the Recovery Appliance exceeded customer targets with no tuning.

RASTAT utility

The rastat utility is a new tool to generate statistics about the performance of Recovery Appliance.

This rastat.pl will be in the /opt/oracle.RecoveryAppliance/client folder of the compute nodes.

```
perl rastat.
pl --test=<options> --rasys=<string> --catalog=<string>

--filesize=<size>M --chunksize=<size>M --diskgroup=<string>
--parms=<string>

--oracle_home=<string> --oracle_sid=<string>
```

The key options are:

1. NETBACKUP measures the network performance of a protected database sending backup byte streams to the Recovery Appliance. This requires catalog parameter also to be specified.

2. NETRESTORE measures the network performance of a protected databases receiving backup byte streams from the Recovery Appliance. This requires catalog parameter also to be specified.

3. ASMREAD measures the disk I/O performance of the Recovery Appliance reading from an ASM disk group. This requires diskgroup & rasys parameters also to be specified.

4. ASMWRITE measures the disk I/O performance of the Recovery Appliance writing to an ASM disk group. This requires diskgroup & rasys parameters also to be specified.

The parms parameter specifies the location of libra.so file and the wallet information.

The default file size is 1024M.

INDEX

U

W

Printed in the United States
By Bookmasters